FREE BOOTS &
BACK-TO-BACKS

Maureen Harvey was born in 1946, and spent her childhood in a terraced back-to-back house on Arthur Street in Birmingham's Small Heath. Although this type of housing was deemed unsatisfactory under the Public Health Act as early as the 1870s, Maureen lived there with her parents and six other siblings until she was eleven, when they moved to a new home in the suburb of Sheldon. At the age of thirteen she had her first Saturday job at a hair salon on Coventry Road, and when she left school at fifteen, the owner offered her a fully paid hairdressing apprenticeship. She thrived in the profession and by the age of twenty was working as a senior hairdresser. In 1967 she married her husband Ray and had two children.

She opened her first salon, 'Ahead of Style', in Birmingham in 1983, and ran her last, 'The Hair Company' in Kings Heath, in partnership with her daughter Michelle, from 1995 to 2001. Maureen never imagined that she and her family would experience great tragedy in their own lives, which led to her writing her first book, *Pure Evil*. This, her second book, recounts her childhood growing up in the back-to-backs. She has three grandchildren and five great-grandchildren.

Charlotte Browne was born in 1980 and knew from a young age that she would probably end up working with words. She has worked as a journalist for a number of publications, from *The Independent* to *Prima*, and also in content marketing, as well as writing for organisations within the not-for-profit and charity sectors. She can talk at great length about her favourite band, Pink Floyd, and is probably at her happiest walking the Cornish countryside, swimming in the sea or when a DJ drops 'Chic' at a party. She probably couldn't write or live without music and loves playing her favourite songs on piano. She lives in South London.

FREE BOOTS & BACK-TO-BACKS

Memories of a 1950s Childhood

MAUREEN HARVEY

with Charlotte Browne

JOHN BLAKE

Published by John Blake Publishing,
3 Bramber Court, 2 Bramber Road,
London W14 9PB, England

www.johnblakebooks.com

www.facebook.com/johnblakebooks 🔳
twitter.com/jblakebooks 🔳

First published in paperback in in 2018

ISBN: 978-1-78606-867-5

British Library Cataloguing-in-Publication Data:

A catalogue record for this book is available from the British Library.

Design by www.envydesign.co.uk

Printed and bound in Great Britain by Clays Ltd, St Ives plc

1 3 5 7 9 10 8 6 4 2

Papers used by John Blake Publishing are natural, recyclable products made
from wood grown in sustainable forests. The manufacturing processes conform
to the environmental regulations of the country of origin.

Every attempt has been made to contact the relevant copyright-holders, but
some were unobtainable. We would be grateful if the appropriate people could
contact us.

John Blake Publishing is an imprint of Bonnier Publishing
www.bonnierpublishing.com

Contents

Introduction   ix

1   Dead-End Kids, Community and Our
Very Own Resident Midwife and Doctor   1

2   Mom and Dad's Wedding Photo,
Relatives and Family Ghosts   29

3   My Siblings and an Unconventional
Wartime Birth   49

4   Clip Round the Ear 'Oles and School
Discipline   61

5   The Club and Rent Man, Meddling Nuns
and Dodging the School Board Man   79

6   Down the Coal 'Ole, Queuing for Coal
and a Fancy New Tiled Grate   87

7   Coronation Day, Our Brand-New Telly
and Grabbing a Tanner for the Meter   97

8   Green Lane Bath House and Library   117

9   Friday Night is Bath Night   125

10 Rescuing Dad's Suit from the Pawn Shop,
    Visiting the Moneylender and Witnessing
    Chicken Slaughter   135

11 Painting My Room Pink and Making the
    Most of Cardboard   145

12 Wash Day in the Brewus   157

13 Bombsites and Collecting Fuel for
    Bonfire Night   167

14 Freezing Cold Winters, Fog and Smog and
    Joey Ellis's Magic Wand   175

15 Polio and a Convalescence Trip to Devon   187

16 Christmas and Sixpence Scams   213

17 The Bull Ring Market, Barrow Boys and the
    City of a Thousand Trades   221

18 Mom's Stockings Save the Day on Our
    Family Holiday to Weston-super-Mare   233

19 Touting for Business at The Blues,
    Getting Caught Scrumping and Teenage
    Heartthrob Tommy Steele   243

20 Leaving Childhood Behind and Moving
    to Sheldon   253

21 Earning My Own Wage as a Hairdresser
    and Meeting My Husband Ray   265

I dedicate this book in loving memory to you, Mom. I wish you were still here to tell me to 'Get up the dancers!' But you're not, so I'll have to wait to tell you in person how much I love, appreciate and respect you for the wonderful upbringing you gave us all. You faced stresses and strains as a mother that I never had to. But you still taught us the importance of integrity, honesty and kindness – a priceless gift.

To my dear Auntie Lil – thank you for teaching me that time really is the best gift you can give someone you love. You are now with your dear sister Annie. Give her my love.
And to the grandmother I never got to know – I'm sorry that secrets kept us apart for so long. I wish we had spent more precious time together. You are not forgotten.
Love always, Maureen Ann

Above all, I would like to thank Jordan, my wonderful grandson, who gave me the inspiration to write this book. For asking me questions about what it was like growing up in my large family in the back-to-backs, during the late 1940s and early 1950s. He asked so many times and never tired, and he wrote about me in his school English compositions.
Thank you Jordan, for your support and endless love.
Nan xx

Also my beautiful daughter and best friend Michelle, for all your help, love, guidance and never-ending support. Love always, Mom xx

My husband Ray, for his patience, love, Maureen xx

All my family, love always, xx

Introduction

When the National Trust began its restoration of the back-to-backs on Hurst Street in 2001 they were overwhelmed by the positive response from the public, who donated whatever artefacts they could, even chimneys, to the project. Many who donated had relatives who had grown up in them. Rather than see the last standing terrace of back-to-backs lost forever under a bulldozer, people wanted this part of history brought back to life – along with the stories passed down to them. And this wasn't just for the sake of nostalgia – but out of a need to keep alive the memories of the people who lived there.

Not only do the local Brummie populace want to learn about the squalid and cramped conditions people endured, they want to know about Mr Oldfield who made glass eyes, George Ellis the cork and sock maker and Elizabeth

Manton who ran the Black Lion pub down the street. Or most recently, the West Indian immigrant George Saunders, who ran a successful tailoring business there from the 1970s until restoration began. They recognise it's important to honour them.

And this, for me, has been one of the main reasons I wanted to tell my story of growing up in the back-to-backs down Arthur Street. Yes, I want people to learn about how tough our upbringing could be in our home – where icicles on the insides of the windows were as normal a part of our surroundings as the draw tin we relied on to get our fires going. Or how it felt to be scalded on the side of the tin bath in front of the hearth, or to queue in the cold for the lav by candlelight.

But I also wanted to write this book to tell the stories of the people I knew. Otherwise the only trace they leave are their names, indelibly printed on a census but just names nonetheless – an indication of their existence but little else. That doesn't seem right or fair, especially as so many of these characters left a long-lasting impression on me. They weren't perfect and were forced to scrape by the best they could. But they were kind, helpful, determined and never sought pity. Not that being pitied gets anyone anywhere. We needed support, help and ultimately action – not the embarrassed uncomfortable silence of a copper who dragged us back home for scrumping, or the haughty glare of the school board governor, fed up with having to tick us off for skiving on wash day.

When support was less than forthcoming from outside authorities – although I remember the cod-liver oil and sterilised milk (stera) the state provided with fondness – we helped each other out. Because who, more often than not, ends up helping the poor but the poor themselves? At least, that was the way back then. Our tight-knit community instilled a sense of compassion for others that has stayed with me throughout life.

I grew up in a large family – I was one of nine, though there were seven of us who lived in the back-to-back house. Our dear mother was known as 'Mom'. This was not some Americanism we picked up by the way, but a standard term that's been used for generations throughout the Midlands and parts of Staffordshire. She taught us always to give whatever we had to help others, even our last penny. And this is a value she nurtured in us early, which has stayed with me throughout life. If I go on holiday with my husband Ray, we'll invariably return with an empty suitcase – literally giving the shirts off our backs.

Although Mom scrimped and saved as much as she could to provide for us, we learnt to rely on ourselves and realised early on that you get what you work for – something that has helped us all to succeed. We climbed out of poverty by our own efforts because no one ever let us sit around or feel sorry for ourselves. We were always on the lookout for new ways to raise cash from the resources around us, which cultivated an entrepreneurial spirit and sense of enterprise within us. I think we owe this in large measure to our backgrounds and the support of our family and friends.

However, I never really realised it at the time but we did need a voice that could speak for us back then. I'm not knocking the intentions or efforts of those that did because they were genuinely altruistic and well-meaning – from the architect Sir Herbert Manzoni who set the slum clearance in motion, to Fred Longden, Labour MP for Birmingham Small Heath, who spoke out against the effects of smoke abatement. The trouble was, they spoke for us but they didn't quite sound like us. Neither did they do enough to consult our communities on how we felt about our neighbourhoods breaking up, although urban regeneration did repair some of the harm this did in later years. One of the reasons why Canon Norman Power – the former vicar of Ladywood and author of *The Forgotten People* – was so deeply respected for his work was because he realised the importance of keeping communities together. His book, published in 1965, focused on the negative impact of newly created high-rise estates in the district. His support for the forgotten people helped give them a voice, too. Women marched in protest from Ladywood to Birmingham Council House, daring to fight the authorities with the same strength they'd wielded with their dolly sticks on wash day in the courtyard. He was prophetic too, warning of segregation in communities and an era when neighbours would barely say hello to each other – a reality for me today.

INTRODUCTION

Even if I had wanted my memories of the back-to-backs to die along with those streets and communities, it would never have been possible anyway. This is thanks to the curiosity of my wonderful grandson Jordan, who inspired me to keep these stories alive and write this book. From the age of eight, he showed a keen interest in my childhood, asking all sorts of questions and reigniting many memories. Unbeknownst to me he'd written some of them down at school – from our tin baths in front of the fire to Mom's backbreaking stints in the brewus. Quite hilariously, his teacher assumed I was either from the Victorian era or not long for this mortal coil – he was surprised to find I was a healthy and hearty woman in her fifties (at the time). Yet another reason I think this story should be told, for many people remain oblivious to just how horrific living conditions could be, even in our very recent history.

In the 1960s and 1970s, the charity Shelter highlighted this problem through a set of harrowing photos – images revealed families that were condemned to live in cellars with rats, without heating, electricity or running water. Many of the children in the photos looked haunted and old before their time. And even now, although children may not be bringing up coal in a bucket from the cellar on their own, figures from 2016 show that child poverty now stands at the highest level since 2010. This is a definite stain on our country, the fifth richest economy in the world.

Sadly, though, I feel children may suffer more today, in some ways, because they don't have the close-knit communities to support them. And I feel the divide in my neighbourhood today that Canon Power predicted all those years ago. I hope that this story of my own childhood is a reminder that even in the worst and hardest of times, it's possible to survive and thrive with the help and support of friends, family and a caring community.

MAUREEN HARVEY

Dead-End Kids, Community and Our Very Own Resident Midwife and Doctor

With a string of sheets hung above to dry or a trail of Terry nappies slung over the fireguard, there's barely a time I can remember when we ever had a clear view of our mantelpiece. There wasn't much that begged for attention when you could see it – just a couple of gnarled-looking candlesticks either end and a box of Dad's England's Glory matches, always at the ready to light one of his Woodbines or Craven A (later he smoked Park Drive). However, in amongst these everyday items stood a framed professional portrait of me as a baby at about eight months old. I'd just won first prize in the *Evening Mail* Baby Contest. Forever on the lookout for new ways to raise cash, I suspect Mom's main motivation for taking a punt on her bonnie-looking baby was for the money, rather than any proud motherly instinct to celebrate my looks – she was known for making beautiful babies so they weren't a rarity as such in our household. Still, her confidence in our good genes paid off and the picture always took pride of place at the hearth, even if it was hidden most of the time by more pressing day-to-day domestic concerns.

Born in March 1946, I was part of the baby boomer generation – a symbol of a fresh start that coincided with a wave of post-war hope and optimism, eventually to usher in the 'most of our people have never had it so good' years, all but a decade later. Of course I had no understanding of this at the time, sitting on the studio floor with the photographer pointing his lens at me.

I look pretty unfazed by my moment of stardom too. I'm clutching a penguin – who knows where that came from? – and staring off to some distraction or other, perhaps Mom beaming proudly. If I'd known then that having your picture taken was a rare occurrence, I might have revelled in the limelight a bit more. Especially as, one of nine children, it was rare any of us got special attention or focus.

The photo is grainy and has nothing of the clarity of today's digitally enhance pictures but yes, with my big brown eyes, button nose and cherubic round face, I do look pretty, sitting there contentedly in the gorgeous knitted jacket my dear Auntie Lil had made.

I often wonder about the competition I was up against. Where were the other baby girls from? Some of the posh houses down Coventry Road perhaps? In some ways rationing was a great leveller. In terms of diet, no baby was particularly better off than the next, regardless of his or her postcode, but it often strikes me when I see this picture, would anyone, looking at this cherubic face with it all ahead of her, ever have reduced this baby to a 'dead-end kid' once they knew my address? 3/84 Arthur Street, to be precise.

I wouldn't have known sitting there. Nor could I predict the tough years in front of me, the hard times living in Birmingham's Small Heath back-to-backs, where the phrase 'Most of our people have never had it so good' would have many in our neighbourhood fighting back tears of bitter irony. But 'dead-end kids' was one of the phrases we used to hear filtering down from the outside world, along with the smog and fog that billowed around our courtyard. We might have been labelled 'dead-end' but within those streets were some of the most alive people I've ever met. Despite the everyday hardships they faced, they created places that could be called home in the toughest of circumstances – they worked all hours to spare themselves from being evicted, from conditions so squalid it seems unbelievable that people still lived in them even fifty years ago.

And although many may have thought our fate was sealed from our humble beginnings, those days were some of the freest times in my memories, where our imaginations soared above the limitations of the brick walls – of those two-up, two-down jerry-built constructions (under pressure to build as many houses as possible in as short amount of time at maximum profit, builders tended to use the cheapest, inadequate or insufficient materials) – as we scurried from bombsites to neighbours' trees scrounging for apples, narrowly missing electrocution on the railway lines or laughing at the black ink on our bums from the makeshift newspaper toilet roll. And I can say with pride we never paid much heed to any damning indictments – we've all gone on to 'better ourselves', certainly in terms of material wealth and social status.

I don't know how conscious a decision this was for us all, it wasn't something we discussed openly as kids. As I played with my doll's house I always dreamed of owning a string of shops one day. But either way, all nine of us went on to create our own businesses and forge successful careers. None of our kids knew what it was to grow up in a house without central heating, where it was so cold icicles of up to three feet formed on the inside of windows or to use a bucket in the night because we couldn't face the outside toilet by candlelight again. However, they also never learnt how to pool all available resources to make a go-kart out of scraps of wood, or fix a leaking roof at short notice, a skill that has instilled a sense we'll be able to stand on our own two feet wherever we are in the world, yet always appreciate what we have.

We've all wanted our kids to be as warm, safe and protected as possible but I wouldn't change my formative years in the back-to-backs for anything. In fact, even as I look around my own beautiful home, with its pristine cream sofa suite, I maintain I'd still go back tomorrow. The Victorians condemned them way back. The Public Health Act meant they were deemed unsatisfactory as far back as 1875 and no more were built, though people still lived in them and they were our home. Of course, part of this wish to return is the joy at the thought of seeing my family again – to know Mom is waiting for me with the tea, to brace myself for my eldest brother Dennis to leap out at me or to find out that another brother, David, has got himself another clip round the ear 'ole for taking the clock apart again, so keen was he to find out how it worked. But as much as anything, I think it's for the community spirit – alive within me still, though the homes that cultivated it have long been demolished. Just to hear Nancy Nee say 'Alright, Pet?' one more time or run like hell from an angry Old Gal Evans, who seemed to have a fast pair of legs on her despite walking with a stick. The thin walls in the original construction of the back-to-backs brought everyone closer together literally, and though there were tough times, it was all we knew and it nurtured a sense of care and compassion within our neighbourhood I've not experienced since.

The restored back-to-backs at the National Trust site on Hurst Street are now a museum, their restoration completed in 2001. They are the only remaining example of the back-to-backs in the city, with the majority destroyed by the late sixties. They present a rosy, almost picturesque view of life back then that differs quite remarkably from my memories of Arthur Street. Still one of the longest streets in Birmingham, it is but a half-hour walk from Hurst Street, which forms part of the area that makes up Small Heath in East Birmingham. Now a suburb, it was transformed in the last quarter of the nineteenth century from an area of agricultural land to one of urban development. In 1863 Small Heath and Sparkbrook station was built to serve the new Birmingham Small Arms factory in Armoury Road, which began in 1861. Then in 1893 Small Heath Library and Baths was built and by 1906 the whole area was built up around the entire length of Coventry Road, or 'The Cov', where its reputation for being the cosmopolitan shopping area that it's known for today was already taking shape, with lively butcher's and grocery shops.

Before you enter the back-to-backs in Hurst Street, what first struck me is that there was a wrought-iron gate in an oval-shaped doorway to welcome visitors to the front of the 'entry'. This was the name for the alleyway down the side of every back-to-back street that led into the courtyard which the back-to-backs surrounded – there was no such welcoming addition for us back in the day. As you walk into the courtyard on Hurst Street today, it almost looks inviting, with its renovated red brick façade – pot plants wave in the breeze and tin baths hang on the wall like garden centre trinkets. There were no plants in our courtyard, nor even any trees nearby.

It's only the presence of an old wooden go-kart pulled together from scrap wood and a basic-looking pushchair that looks as though it's sprung from the Victorian Age that contradicts the almost Cotswold-like feel of the place. So too the scattered rubber tyres, lifted from an old bicycle before upcycling became trendy and people recycled materials out of sheer necessity. We were innovating without realising it then, ahead of our time – bicycle tyres became hula hoops, a washing line doubled as a skipping rope, a spare piece of chalk was like gold dust for our Hopscotch game, or an old broken wooden peg could be magically transformed into a dolly. Everything, from cardboard to wood or leather, had the potential for rebirth.

The smells emitting from the 'miskins' have also gone. This was the colloquial term in the West Midlands for the section of yard that was saved for dustbins, but it was also used to describe the toilets. The derivation of the original Anglo-Saxon word is 'mixen' and goes back as far as the nine hundreds. Also long gone is the blanket of smog that would envelope our yard, an accursed by-product of the factories and cars that choked our streets and seeped into our clothing, so overpowering at times that we shuffled along warily like hedgehogs, barely able to see one hand in front of our faces.

As we were guided around our tour most people gasped at the day-to-day horrors that blighted our existence, which we'd come to see as so ordinary – from sagging ceilings to freezing temperatures and the red smudged residues on the ceiling from yet another bed bug we'd splattered with the end of a broom. No one believed me when I said I'd go back tomorrow.

The Arthur Street I remember is completely unrecognisable. Not only are the back-to-backs long gone, they've been replaced with little cul-de-sacs that give a clear view down to my old junior school, Dixon Road, previously obstructed by hundreds of crammed-in streets of housing and factories. You might be forgiven for thinking the Industrial Revolution had never impacted this street though it's integral to understanding the history of the back-to-backs.

I knew and understood very little of this important part of our city's history, though history's fumes continued, not far from my doorstep – there were three or four Lycett's factories in the area that made bicycle accessories and other leather accessories. Nor did I have any concept of the fact it was money-motivated landowners and 'jerry-builders' who had a hand in creating some of the worst features of my slum upbringing, from the sagging ceilings of our bedrooms to the appalling sanitary conditions.

Back in the 1840s, thousands of terraced back-to-back dwellings were thrown up across Birmingham, as quickly and as cheaply as possible, to maximise profit on as small an amount of land as possible. They were built to provide housing for the new working classes, to cater for the huge influxes of people who migrated from the country to the city, looking for work. The cheapest of materials were used, from the bricks to the horsehair to fill the plaster, and even dirt, instead of sand, for their very foundations. False advertising existed even back then and slogans such as 'urban cottages' were used, encouraging the working classes to aspire to communal living, while effectively condemning them to a cramped existence and poor conditions, where disease could spread all too easily. But due to one housing crisis after another, in large part caused by two world wars, many families, including my own, were still carving out their lives in them, one hundred years later.

By the time I was born in 1946 the City Council of Birmingham had acquired 981 acres near the centre of the city. The man behind this was the visionary engineer and architect Herbert Manzoni. His name meant little to those growing up in the backstreets but he was to have a profound effect on both the physical landscape of my city and the lives of people living there within the communities. After he joined the council in 1923 he swiftly became its city engineer and surveyor, propelling its much-needed modernisation in housing forward. His clear authoritative voice rings out in a 1958 film called *City of Birmingham Central Areas - Redevelopment* detailing the regeneration of Birmingham (directed by Sir Herbert Manzoni, CBE, the film can be found on *Regenerating Birmingham, 1955 to 1975*, a 2012 DVD written and directed by Mike Mason). In one scene, the camera pans over an aerial view from St Albans' church tower that overlooks the slum dwellings. It's not a pretty sight to be sure and Manzoni describes the vista as 'frightful, weary, dilapidated'. Indeed, there is little colour to be seen amongst the grey and drudgery but for the flash of a green coat wrapped around a child playing. Manzoni sounds both grave and sad as he outlines the damning statistics – 'the 29,526 dwellings house 102,000 people – 18,000 of these are back-to-back, 20,000 have no separate sanitary accommodation and 4,000 have no internal water supply'.

The view is as depressing as the statistics and I'm not surprised he sounds so dejected. But in amongst the weariness real people still lived and thrived as much as they could. I was one of them, living as he said 'cheek by jowl' with factories, warehouses, scrapyards and bombsites. But I was one of the lucky few who happened to have their own internal water supply. Indeed, we were fortunate in that indoor plumbing had moved on a little from the Victorian days of collecting from wells – our nearest would have been at Ladywell Walk, beneath the Hippodrome Theatre, a good half-hour away from where we lived.

Birmingham was actually the first city to have water pumped into houses although many back-to-backs still relied solely on using an outdoor hand pump. Unlike our Victorian counterparts, we didn't live in the cellar either, although Mom and Dad remembered nights cowering down there during the Blitz. Some enemies last a generation, though. Because the builders used dirt in the foundations when they originally built them, our closest neighbours were bugs nestling in the horsehair amongst the plaster – they loved those gaps and we never quite won the battle to eradicate them.

Despite Manzoni's plans to modernise back in 1946, it wouldn't be till 1959, when I turned thirteen, that demolition and clearance of the streets I grew up in would begin. By then a huge chunk of my childhood had been spent there. In the subsequent years, many thousands would be moved out to surrounding redeveloped central areas or huge estates. This solved the problems of poor and inadequate housing and sanitation but brought different and, in some ways, more complex difficulties. Where kids once played out late till all hours on the surrounding streets they were now confined to high-rise flats where they got under the feet of their parents, who were also trapped and isolated. Because one thing's for sure, despite the squalor, supportive communities grew out of those original neighbourhoods and it's these I remember, even if the houses themselves have long gone.

My family, the Rainbirds, lived at 3 of 84 on Arthur Street. This meant we were the third house of 84 that was made up of eight terraced houses built back-to-back – so-called because each house shared a spine wall with another house facing in the opposite direction. Ours faced onto the courtyard so our door was technically the back door.

We had two entries in our terrace – damp, unkempt and uninviting, these were brick-covered alleyways without any child-proof locks or gates. There were entries all the way down the entire street separating houses and it was these that you walked down to, to enter either the courtyard – or 'yard' as we affectionately knew it – or to gain entrance to the houses on the back. We loved to race up and down these and they were a brilliant place for Hide and Seek too.

To our left were two other houses with families – the Clarkes and the Fosters. To our right were the Bottrells. Their homes were practically identical to ours in that they had back doors. This meant we paid less rent than those with a front door, a fact that hadn't changed since Victorian times. We backed onto the Jeys (who were my Uncle Ernie and his wife Auntie Lily and their two kids, Martin and Heather). They had a front door, as did the Nees, on the other side of the entry – they shared a back wall with the Bottrells.

Interestingly, as far back as the 1840s the Reverend Charles, one of the local clergy, talked about unspoken hierarchies within the back-to-backs that were often reflected in the rental prices. If your home faced the street and you had the privilege of your own front door – which normally included a side door too, backing onto the scullery – it was considered a bit 'posh', even in our day. However, I never felt anyone in our yard got above his station for this additional luxury. Whether a front or back door, no one liked an unexpected knock on it – could it be the club or rent man wanting money? It was an uncomfortable sound that many of us dreaded. More often than not we would all just walk in and out of each other's houses without so much as a by your leave – it wasn't as if many of us had anything worth stealing! So a knock wasn't always a welcome sign.

As the Reverend observed though, the 'yard' – the central communal point that stored both the miskins and brewhouses ('brewuses') for washing – was 'a great leveller'. And he was right: in our yard we were all equal and tackled the same problems – whether battling to dry our sheets in our common enemy, the British weather, or swilling our 'po' in the outdoor tap. Here, any final airs or graces you wished to uphold were almost certainly washed away in those everyday domesticities – there was little you could hide in broad daylight within the community. Although there is also some irony in the Reverend's statement too because the yard was anything but level – inferior outdated Victorian drainage meant that water never poured away properly, just one of the many problems no one was ever in any hurry to fix for us. Indeed, wars were fought and governments came and went, but throughout those one hundred years little changed within our functioning amenities era. From the copper boiler in the brick house to the plumbing in the outside loo, these facilities spanned the generations.

If you look at pictures from the 1940s of a family supping tea in their living room, little differentiates the scene from the Victorian period other than the women's shorter skirts, flowery fabrics and hair turbans.

The Clarkes, Fosters and Bottrells were much smaller-sized families than ours. Mr and Mrs Clarke were a pleasant couple with two children in their late teens, Margaret and Billy. We directly shared one wall with them to our left and as you might expect, those walls were thin – thick walls had not been a priority for the jerry-builders.

I felt for them at times, for the close proximity to our family with the amount of racket we kids often made, especially when Dad finally acquired an accordion that he loved practising on – one of his most prized possessions. We definitely won in the sound wars but we could sometimes hear them too, talking late into the night, and every Sunday lunchtime without fail, Mr Clarke would put his favourite radio programme on – the *Billy Cotton Bandshow*. Other times you could hear one of them weeing in the bucket late at night, as though it was right up to your ear, and if Uncle Ernie and Auntie Lily were having a row you'd soon know about it – here, it was the norm to know other people's business.

Because the Fosters were on the other side of the entry our interaction with them was fairly minimal. It was the Bottrells and the Nees that we formed a particularly close bond with, not least because Mr Bottrell became our very own resident dentist and Nancy Nee our very own resident midwife.

Variation in design was not at the top of the list of the jerry-builders' priorities either. All the houses in our court were one room deep and followed a two-up, two-down model spread out over three storeys – the ground floor combining the living space and scullery, with bedrooms spread over the remaining two, normally culminating in an attic room at the top. Our small living room, the main family communal area, was approximately nine by ten feet, with a well-worn wooden table with a chenille tablecloth that normally covered it, two un-matching armchairs and a handmade rag rug that my dad had created, placed in front of the black-leaded grate coal fire. Mom also had a sideboard where she kept important papers and sometimes clothes, which she would wrap in brown paper and lavender to keep them smelling fresh.

The scullery was so small that if there were two of you in there you couldn't move – generally, it was the coolest place in the house. With no fridge or, indeed, any mod cons, this was the place where we kept our lard, or any food that we needed to keep as chilled as possible. Above the gas cooker, our one gas-fuelled appliance in the house, Dad put up shelves he'd made, where we kept a couple of pots and pans, cups and plates.

Obviously we had no back door or a window as this was part of the wall we shared with the Jeys. From there, a medium-sized industrialised sink hung by its hinges on the back of a damp wall, which had paint peeling off it. The loud banshee-type wail that accompanied every turn of the copper tap was a reminder of just how ancient our plumbing was. Still, we had running water, if only cold. From there, concrete steps led down to the cellar, where the coal was kept. Cold, dark and musty, it was home to many happy families of mice, rats and beetles, which we called 'black bats', living down there. Sometimes they crept up to the house to say hello.

From the living room was a tiny flight of winding staircases leading up to the first floor. There was no handrail to guide you, and each step barely measured a foot across so it was something of a tiptoeing act to get up and down our stairs, even with small feet! On the first floor was a small landing, of only about two or three feet across, where a bucket was strategically placed in the winter months for last-minute sanitary purposes. Mom and Dad's bed took up most of the space in their room but in the corner was a single, where the youngest children would sleep in later years. It's also where I slept for a while once I'd reached an age that my parents deemed it unsuitable for me to sleep in the same bed as my brothers anymore. For years up until that point I slept in the attic room with three of my brothers, four of us to a bed, topping and tailing. This was one of the rooms where the poor foundations of the original building tended to reveal themselves the most – with its sagging ceiling, horrific damp and mould, as well as gaps where water could often seep through.

There was also very little available light to infiltrate these houses and lift people's spirits. Ours was no different – three windows of not more than four by two feet across, plus the courtyard and other houses blocked what little light did reach us. Opposite our row of houses, on the other side of the courtyard, was another set of terraced back-to-backs. Here lived the Ellis family and the Griffins

– the Griffins were an elderly couple but the Ellises also had a son and daughter at home, Margaret and George. Although the courtyard was a great leveller, they were considered a little more well-to-do than us for the simple fact that the Ellises kept pigeons for racing and the Griffins had chickens. With these luxuries they had their own eggs and of course, with no children, fewer mouths to feed.

When Mom peeled the potatoes and vegetables we used to fight over the peelings because if we took them up the yard to Mrs Griffin or Mrs Ellis they would sometimes give us a penny for them, as they were not so poor as us. They would boil them up and mix them in with the feed for their chickens and pigeons.

Between the houses on the opposite side was an open entry leading to more back-to-backs and another, smaller yard. Our yard had the accolade of being the biggest, with the Victorian hand pump, our very own water feature, at the centre of it all. On either side were two brewhouses, each containing a copper boiler set in a brick surround used on wash day. In between each one of these were the final additions to our Victorian kingdom: the outside toilets and miskins.

Behind the Griffins lived Old Gal Evans. Yes, not the nicest of names, but to us kids, anyone over the age of thirty looked old to us – I don't think we ever called that to her face, though! She was probably only in her fifties but of course to us she seemed ancient. She was like something of a battle-axe caricature out of a Dickens story – permanently attached to her walking stick, which I suspect was more of an accessory to wave angrily in the air at us kids when we caused mischief than to actually assist her mobility.

We were terribly naughty though at times. 'Knock Door Run' was one of our favourite games in those days to terrorise the neighbours with. Most of them were quite good-natured about it and would be relieved to find no one at the door when they answered – well, at least it wasn't the club or rent man asking for payment! I'm afraid Old Gal Evans was one of our favourite recipients, not least because it wound her up to boiling point – she would call out all kinds of names and if she caught up with one of us, she'd get a few good thwacks in for good measure. We used to laugh and say, 'God, she runs faster without her stick!'

I would eventually have a closer connection to her than I realised though, which I discovered years later. When I first started dating my husband Ray in 1962 I found out that his sister Betty had been adopted by none other than Old Gal Evans. In those days it was quite a common arrangement for childless women to adopt their nieces or nephews as it gave them a chance to have their own child to love and care for. It probably sounds a little strange now that people would give up their own kids but as they tended to have more children back then, they often concluded their child would be better off financially and have more care. In some ways it could be argued that this was quite a selfless act.

Such was the case with Ray's sister Betty. Their mom

lived in Warstock in the southern suburbs and had eight children – Ray was the youngest. She lost her husband, Herbert Harvey, to a heart attack when Ray was only six months old and thought that four-year-old Betty would be better off with her aunt. Betty loved her aunt and appreciated the extras she was able to give her but years later it did cause a rift between the family. When I talked to Betty about this she said she felt that although she was grateful for a good upbringing, with more material blessings, she'd missed bonding with her brothers and sisters. She felt guilt too that at times there was more to go round for her. If you've experienced a stark difference in upbringing it can create a divide that's hard to cross.

Betty went on to marry and have two children. Years later, she was delighted to find out that I was courting Ray, when to her great surprise she came to visit her mom in Warstock and saw us holding hands right there in the living room. By this point I was sixteen and living in the suburb of Sheldon – it had been at least five years since I'd left the back-to-backs. We caught up on all the family gossip and needless to say, Ray couldn't get a word in that day.

It was strange to discover that Ray had been visiting his sister and aunt down Arthur Street all those years and that our paths had likely crossed at some point, also interesting to hear his thoughts on the back-to-backs there. Ray had grown up in relative luxury in Warstock – they'd never gone to bed hungry, thanks in part to the fact that he and his brothers worked down the market. He used to detest visiting Old Gal Evans in the back-to-backs – he wiggled his nose when I asked him why and said, 'It smelt funny.' He hated the intense smell of damp. It was often so cold in the houses that people kept any doors and windows shut so there was never an opportunity to ventilate the rooms properly. But most of all, Ray recalls the overpowering aroma of DDT, an extremely potent chemical so strong that it was used in the second half of World War II to control malaria and typhus amongst civilians and troops. It was also our trusted ally against the bugs that infiltrated our homes. Though the battle against them was rarely won it kept them at bay for short bursts. We bought DDT from the Co-op and would spray it everywhere, using a hand pumper mercilessly. Any who escaped that fate were bludgeoned on the ceiling with a broom. I got very used to the smell, but Ray hated it so much that he ended a date he once had at the pictures with a girl who lived on one of the back-to-backs' streets – it was obviously a smell strong enough to kill off any romance! Lucky enough for me, I suppose.

John and Rose Bottrell ('Mr and Mrs' to us, of course, as in those days we never called our elders by their first names) lived next door to us, to our right. Their house was on the same side as us, but we were separated by the entry. So, their front door was also technically the back door. They had a son and a daughter but they were quite a number of years older so never played with us and the other kids in the yard. Because they had fewer children the family seemed to have more space and their home always seemed a lot cosier and less ramshackle. If we needed to borrow or scrounge a tanner (sixpence; 2.5p) we'd go there first as we knew we'd get the kindest reception.

John always wore a checked flat cap and had a quizzical yet mischievous glint in his eye. I think I trusted him instantly. Looking back, he reminds me quite a lot of Clegg from the BBC sitcom *Last of the Summer Wine*, that similar self-effacing humour with a willingness to stay positive and never take life too seriously. He always saw the funny side of things, even when the fog was at its worse or the pipes froze in the outside toilet for the third time in one winter – he was a saint in my eyes. Rose had a similar temperament that brimmed over with proper Brummie hospitality. Rosy-cheeked and jovial, she always had a kind word or smile and was willing to put the kettle on for anyone who popped by, while she clucked about in her apron. She was friendly without being nosey and not dissimilar to Ivy from *Last of the Summer Wine* – she called a spade a spade but was ultimately kind-hearted. I remember them as some of the sweetest and kindest of our neighbours and many years later, I still recall their gentle yet easy-going manner with us.

It was Mr Bottrell's breezy and fun way with children that led to him becoming our stand-in dentist. I don't think it was ever a job he planned to sign up for but it started when I was playing round there one day and one of my teeth started bleeding. 'It's loose!' I shrieked. It was my first one so I was excited, if a little scared too.

He was as calm as anything and said: 'If you can be really, really brave, which I know you can, I'll take it out for you. The fairies will come tonight if you leave it under your pillow and they'll be so impressed with how courageous you are, they'll give you some money in return.'

Well, I couldn't believe it! I was so excited that real fairies were coming to see me in our attic. 'Gosh,' I thought, 'I'd better tidy it up!'

Mr Bottrell started to quiz me about whether or not I liked fairies and if I had met any. How many had I seen, what did they look like and where did they live? Intrigued, he wanted to hear what I had to say. I'd never seen any in the back-to-backs but I liked to imagine they lurked in the scullery or popped up from the cellar at night. That was one way to explain away the scratching on the flagstone flooring when we lay awake in bed at night.

Either way, Mr Bottrell's tender fun talk helped boost my confidence throughout. As he gently tied a piece of cotton around my tooth, he praised my courage once more then distracted me with: 'Oh my, would you look at that big black spider over there on the wall!' before he pulled it out. It was over in no time. After wrapping my tooth up in a piece of cotton wool, he placed it in a matchbox as though it were a precious gemstone. He then gave me a Victory liquorice lozenge to wash away any pain, which left me grimacing a little.

I was awake most of the night in anticipation, as were Dennis and David. They teased me and said there were no such things as fairies, but the next morning I was overjoyed to see the tooth had gone, replaced with a couple of pennies. Well, that was it. My brothers wanted to sign him up as their dentist too, seeing as he was special enough to have a direct line to the fairies. So, between the ages of six and eight, when all our baby teeth were coming through, he was our go-to man for all dentistry requirements, not least because he seemed to have a direct hotline. Us kids were always on the lookout for new money making schemes and it proved a lucrative one over these years.

But I really remember Mr Bottrell because he also indulged our childlike imaginations and further inspired my fascination with fairies. He brought it all to life with his make-believe that would soften the pain of having your tooth pulled out – from the final last few wiggles to dislodge it or a more dramatic root-wrench involving the old door handle trick.

It's funny now to think I had no idea what he did for a living. Although we were so close as neighbours physically there were certain aspects of people's 'business' you just didn't enquire about. Interesting that I still remember him so vividly at seventy-one. I think it's not only the fact he cheered me up and made me laugh but the time and attention he gave to us because we never felt as though we were too much trouble. Even when we occasionally interrupted his tea, he never told us to go away. He'd take one look at our traumatised faces and say, 'OK, remember how brave you are, this won't take a minute.' Once the mayhem had passed, he'd carry on eating his dinner.

My later experiences with a real dentist were far more traumatic and a lot less pleasant! Despite overindulging occasionally in sherbet and kali dips as a child, I still have all my own teeth today, though. ('Kali' is local and North of England slang for a crystal form of sherbet, which came in different colours and flavours.)

Bless Mom too. Children's teeth don't account for a strict budget but there would always be a penny or two under the pillow, any time of the day or week. I think she borrowed money occasionally to make sure we got our visit from the tooth fairy but she never failed us. Little did I know that Mr Bottrell sometimes helped Mom out too – he really was kind.

Nancy Nee lived on the other side of our entry. Her house faced onto the front of Arthur Street and she also had a side door, although she blocked this up to give her more cupboard room space in the scullery, which it backed onto. With or without a front or side door, she certainly hadn't acquired any airs or graces throughout her life either. She was strong and solid, but slim with it. Her face tended to be fixed in quite a stern expression that warned you not to 'push it' at twenty paces, although it would relax a little when she bent over the palings (fencing) at the first hint of a bit of gossip. Most of the time she wore her straight brown hair in rollers to her chin, wrapped up in a turban, as was the way with so many women of that time. I often used to wonder what they actually rolled their hair for, so often was it tightly bundled up in them – I even had a few neighbours who wore them all day to my wedding!

Nancy had three children – Ann, Valerie and Mickey. I was close friends with Valerie, who was in the same year as me, but we would always hang around with her older sister, Ann, like a little troupe. They both had sweet, open and oval-shaped faces. And as was often the way then, encouraging individuality in children wasn't particularly encouraged so, only a year apart, they were usually dressed in the same flowery pinafores with the same bob hairdo. Barbara, my younger sister, and I suffered exactly the same grievance as we grew up together. Mickey was very strong and good-looking, with dark curly hair and cheeky, glinting eyes that were black as coal. He was a bit of a rogue, though Ann and Valerie really looked up to him, and got into trouble quite a bit with the law, but none of us kids ever knew what for – Nancy loved a good gossip but woe betide anyone who ever dared talk about her son! She brought the three of them up completely on her own. There was never any sign of their father, but the reasons for his absence weren't ever openly discussed, not that I ever sensed any stigma surrounding the fact she was a single mom. She definitely wasn't one to wallow in this either – she was one of the toughest, most indomitable women I've ever known, yet also one of the kindest.

Though she had very little herself, she helped the

neighbours out in many different ways, from small gestures such as sharing a bit of sugar for a cup of tea to providing practical support for expectant mothers. This was her speciality and she was the first woman we called on when Mom went into labour, well before the actual midwife arrived. These are the moments that still astound me when I look back on them now.

My memories of Nancy are often triggered by the BBC drama *Call the Midwife*. She would literally drop everything to help out – whether that was the coal bucket, a roast chicken or a hearth brush. The sight of her running up our stairs is still clear in my mind.

While Dad made off to the pub to await any news, Nancy brought peace and calm to an extremely fraught situation. A man's presence at childbirth was certainly not deemed necessary in those days – if anything it was viewed as a hindrance. Not even walking up and down the corridor with a fretful expression served much purpose; ordinarily he'd just head for the pub.

Nancy was the strong one in those circumstances. She'd tell us to put the water on, and fetch towels and sheets. Nothing was sterilised then, so everything needed to be boiled. We'd be upstairs waiting for the baby to arrive, cowering by the door while Mom screamed to the heavens. It was upsetting to hear and I remember vowing, 'I'm never having a baby!' Mom would even shout things out like 'Maureen, don't ever let a boy touch you!' This didn't make much sense to me at the time as I thought you could get pregnant from the toilet seat – yes, sex education at that time involved little more than showing tadpoles going at it. My generation remained pretty innocent, even up until the age of sixteen (the legal age of consent).

Afterwards, everyone would buy Dad a drink in the pub, which was about as celebratory as the occasion ever got – well, it was such a regular occurrence! We were obviously all very happy when the baby arrived healthy. Out of nine children we all survived and as far as I know, Mom had no miscarriages, so I feel Nancy Nee's emergency care and tender soothing attention made all the difference.

2

Mom and Dad's Wedding Photo, Relatives and Family Ghosts

On a page of the *Birmingham Mail*, dated 30 January 1943, there is a flash of normality, perhaps even hope, in amongst the war reports that blighted readers' newspapers during those times. Surrounded by stories of Hitler's latest speech, prisoners breeding rabbits in Japanese war camps and even young doctors resigning in a BMA revolt is a picture of my parents on their wedding day. There wasn't much time for romantic gestures between Mom and Dad when I was growing up – fanning the fire flames with a draw tin, rather than the flames of romance took precedence. But there is a glint of it here in this picture, which is one of the reasons why I love it so much.

As I said, it was rare to see Dad make dramatic romantic gestures but there's a hint of pride and perhaps even humility in his eyes here. It's obvious they're both posing for the photographer, who has clearly directed their positions. He is perched on my Auntie Lil's garden fence separating 22 and 24 Orpwood Wood, in the suburb of Yardley, where they both grew up. Dad lived at number 22, Mom at 24 – she was literally the girl next door. They'd become so close they were almost like 'brother and sister', as Dad says in the story. He's poised and handsome in his sailor suit and hat, with his dark wavy hair that we all inherited. And as posed as the photo is, there is a genuine smile spreading across Mom's face as she leans forward, gazing tenderly into my dad's eyes. As is fitting for the times, her wedding dress is no more glamorous than an office pinafore, pulled over a silk, cream, long-sleeved, high-neck top with the hemline sitting just below the knee. As was typical of these austere times, materials were used for essentials, such as parachutes or office uniforms, although during the war wedding gowns were sometimes made of parachute silk.

She looks as though she's pushed the boat out on her patent footwear, though – *very* posh! Her hair is also worn in the medium-length fashion of the day, with a slight curl at the bottom and on the top – no doubt expertly waved with a hot poker as usual on that day, if not by Auntie Lil, most probably herself. With her clear porcelain skin, open, oval-shaped face and sparkling eyes, and beautifully thick and dark wavy hair, Mom was incredibly pretty. I think Dad often feared she would attract too much attention down the pub and never encouraged her to wear much make-up.

The photo also reflects the rather kitsch headline which reads in bold capitals – 'GARDEN-FENCE LOVER WAS TOO SHY TO PROPOSE'. Shyness was never a characteristic I ever really associated with Dad and he must have had some nerve to balance for that long on Auntie Lil's palings. But there's a charming tone to this story of two lovebirds, only eighteen and nineteen at the time. As you look at them both, you wouldn't think there was a war on or that my dad had been on one of the boats involved during the Battle of the River Plate, the first proper battle of the Royal Navy of World War II, barely three years before. Looking back, it's highly likely that he lied about his age – whether out of intense patriotism on his part to fight for his country or the fact he just wanted to get away from the stepfather he detested, I can't be sure. However, he would have seen some sights at the tender age of fifteen, things that were never discussed with us.

The story goes on to detail how they had been 'courting over the garden fence for two years' and that while Joe had come home on a week's leave the previous Friday, Ruby also had a week's leave from her job as a munitions worker – taking time out from the war effort to be with him. It goes on to say they could have married on the first day of his leave, but the sailor was so shy of asking Ruby that he did not take her to the Register Office until the day he was due to go back.

Mom is quoted as saying: 'It was a fortnight ago when Joe first asked me to marry him. But he kept saying he did not want to rush it.' I can't help but chuckle at this. The lack of rush may have been down to the cost – seven shillings and sixpence (37.5p) in those days for a wedding licence (quite a princely sum in those days and equivalent to nearly £8 today). If you're a fan of bingo you'll know they often call out after the number 76 – 'Was she worth it?' in reference to an old joke about whether or not the bride was worth the cost of the licence. Dad never did give a definitive answer on that one but I certainly think she more than was!

There was also another reason to rush, at least in an era when illegitimacy was still frowned upon. Yes, at the time Mom was at least a month into her pregnancy with my eldest brother, Dennis (named after one of Dad's brothers, who I think died young). I think they would have married eventually anyway but I've often wondered about Dad's brother, Bill. He was also in the Navy and died near the beginning of the war but Mom's eyes always twinkled a little whenever he was mentioned. I think she may have had a soft spot for him – amazing what kids pick up, even when few words are spoken. We all have a tendency to fill in the gaps, but it was a common occurrence in those days when secrets seemed to stir like whispering autumnal leaves all around us.

I often feel for them both though when I see this picture for they were about to leave behind a relatively safe and comfortable life in that suburban neighbourhood. The UK faced one of its biggest housing crises in both the inter-war and war years – only 500 were built in the country alone between 1939–45. This forced them, as was the case with many young couples, into lodgings before they announced the pregnancy and were moved by the council into our home on Arthur Street, as it was no longer suitable for Mom to stay in their current accommodation with a child on the way. But when she left Orpwood Road, she was also leaving behind one of her greatest supporters in life – Auntie Lil.

Although her elder sister, Lil was more of a mother figure to her. They had lost both their parents so were technically orphans – Auntie Lil at the age of seventeen, Mom at six. They shared the same mother – Lydia Bryan – but had different fathers. Lydia married three times, which was somewhat unheard of for a woman in those days – I hope they were all worth it! Mom's father was George Brewin, Lydia's last husband.

Mom also had another elder brother and sister, Phoebe and Ernie. Their father was Mr Jeys. As you grow up, it's rare that you give much thought to the personal tragedies that befall your parents but my mom certainly had her fair share, far too young. TB is an all but unheard of disease now, but she lost both parents to it.

Born in 1923, my mom, christened Ruby Brewin, was just four when her father, George, died at forty-nine in 1927, and nearly seven when her mother also succumbed to TB only a few years later, in 1930. She also lost her older brother, Joseph, to the disease when she was eleven. People think these diseases died out in the Victorian era but they were still in circulation until injections became routine. I realise how blessed my generation is for the majority of us were fortunate to reap the benefits of so many medical advances. Mom never talked about losing either parent, but Auntie Lil would occasionally say if I pressed her – what a 'lovely woman' she was, but that she, Ernie and Phoebe had all 'tried to bring Mom up well so she would have a good life'. It's only recently, however, that I discovered they also lost a sister through extremely tragic circumstances when they lived in the back-to-backs down Garrison Lane, just off Coventry Road and Arthur Street. (It's at the back of Kingston Pictures and the Birmingham Blues football ground, now notorious for the story of the *Peaky Blinders*' gang, immortalised in the BBC TV series.)

Her name was Annie. Born in 1903, she would have been the eldest and was only twelve when she fell down the narrow dark wooden stairs of their home. When I visited the restored back-to-backs at the National Trust site in Hurst Street, it struck me again what a potential death trap those tiny and winding stairs were. Not that this ever bothered any of my brothers, who came stampeding down them, not a care in the world. But for poor Annie, her fall had fatal consequences. Soon afterwards, she developed a condition called crepitus sternocostoclavicular, a swelling of the brain. She was sent to a Catholic nuns' convalescence home in Gloucester. This was a long way from her family in Birmingham, especially when travel wasn't as accessible, and they couldn't afford to make the journey that often. It's heartbreaking to think of Annie alone, with no family nearby and no one to answer her questions. She died during World War I, in 1916, when thousands of men were literally ploughed into premature mass graves. But Annie was not to have a proper burial either. The end of her life was marked by only a pauper's grave – a fate determined through no fault of her own, but perhaps inevitable for the street she'd been born into.

My middle name is Ann so her story resonates with me so much more now that I have this forgotten piece of the family jigsaw puzzle. I remember as a child that Auntie Lil would often say my full name – 'Maureen Ann' – in her sweet, gentle voice. There is so much more to a name than just a syllable or two – she must have caught a fleeting glimpse of the sister she lost each time she said it. Back then there was barely time for emotions and feelings but you knew they were there, just brimming at the surface. There are no pictures of Annie but my cousin Brian recently found out where her remains are and paid to have them transferred to a proper burial site. I feel proud that her memory was kept alive in some small symbolic way through my name conveying what Auntie Lil or Mom couldn't put into words.

Auntie Lil was a born matriarch, although this was a role thrust upon her in some ways. As well as being mother to Mom, she was a strong, kind and gentle grandmother figure to us all, up until her death. When I was a child, she reminded me a lot of the music-hall act Old Mother Riley, an Irish washerwoman character played hilariously by Arthur Lucan. Funnily enough, she did enjoy a late-night drink in the Irish pubs near Sheldon in her twilight years – my brother Dennis would often see her off home on the night bus. But when she was younger, she had been incredibly beautiful. I remember one particular photo of her when she was slim, with fair skin and a few freckles. With all the selfies nowadays and endless scrutiny of how everyone looks, it's hard to remember a time when photos were still seen as quite rare, unique moments. Her shoulder-length hair was done up, rolled at the sides and under in a pageboy style. It was an unusual colour – a gingery golden hue mixed with a touch of natural blonde. She never had colours on her hair or perms, though she sweetly allowed me to practise on her years later when I was doing my hairdressing apprenticeship.

Born in 1906, she would have been twenty-four when her own mother – Lydia – died. Lil had originally moved into Orpwood Road, in Lea Hall, East Birmingham, when she was pregnant with her son, Ray. We knew very little about what happened to his father. It was frowned upon to ask about things like that, not that this ever stopped me – curious little bugger that I was. The standard answer regarding any man's absences tended to be 'He died in the war'. Probably easier to say than the truth and Auntie Lil was very good at changing the subject on all these topics, asking me to tell her about Brownies or school. And in some ways I think she much preferred being on her own. I hate to think that she suffered any heartbreak, but she was always in a good mood and seemed incredibly grateful for her home in Orpwood Road, where she remained all her life. Her home was a refreshing respite for us because although an ordinary sized house, it seemed like a palace in comparison with what we were used to – it was a home from home.

It had a small hallway, with stairs leading off to two neat little bedrooms. The bathroom was downstairs, off the kitchen. It was narrow, but had a bath that to me seemed very deep in comparison to our tin bath, as well as a small washbasin. I would lay in that bath till the water was cool then top it up with more hot water, just because I could. Auntie Lil used to say, 'How much longer are you gonna stay in that bath, Your Highness? You'll be like a prune if you stay in too long!'

Like us, she had an outdoor toilet and a coal house, but these were joined to the building outside her back door, while her own garden was very long, with a small, low fence on both sides. She kept the lawn trimmed and neat until halfway down, where she let the grass run wild – I loved it as a child because it was knee-high and seemed like a jungle all around me. In the school holidays, the boys would make dens down there and I'd play with my friend June, who lived next door.

Auntie Lil had a remarkable gentleness and patience – I think the only time I tested her was when she tried to teach me to knit or sew. She couldn't understand why I was happy to miss sewing at school – she herself adored crafts. 'Can't or won't?' she would say to me whenever I objected to even threading a needle or sewing on a button.

One of my fondest memories is her teaching me to make pom poms. She would customise almost every item of clothing for us kids with these – from scarves to cardigans and hats, adding her own spark of originality to what would otherwise be an ordinary outfit. People often remember fifties Britain as a grey time but for me, it was punctuated by Auntie Lil's colourful creations. It makes me laugh when I wander around the market now and see what fashionable accessories they've become – she was so en vogue and ahead of her time was Lil, I realise that now.

We would cut two round pieces of cardboard – recycled from anywhere we could find, of course. Sometimes we used the waxed cardboard discs from the tops of milk bottles from school if the teacher let us collect them. After washing them, we'd hold two together, then use wool on a big needle and thread through the hole, round the outer edge and back through the centre. Often we would use lots of different wool colours if we could, although my favourite colour was pink. Then Auntie Lil would cut the wool round the outer edge with the scissors between the two discs and wind a strong thread between them, creating a woolly ball. Sometimes they made good distracting toys for the babies to play with too, if we attached one to the pram. We would also tie old pegs or use cotton reels on string to make rattles.

Although she clearly enjoyed passing down these skills and talents it was also Lil's own way of showing us love. The time she gave me really made a difference – to know that she was interested in me, and my thoughts and feelings. A visit from her to the back-to-backs was always a treat as we knew that she'd bring us something new – either her own knitted creations or second-hand clothes from the market she customised. She'd wash and iron them and turn them up because she'd always buy two sizes bigger to allow for growth. Sometimes I went with her – I loved the noise and bustle as I do today, in amongst throngs of people pushing to get the best prices for their money. If it wasn't clothes she'd bring a homemade fruit cake, Victoria sponge or even a jam roly-poly.

Because she knew Mom was stretched financially, Lil had her little tradition of bringing her own packed lunch with her and continued to do so for years after, even when we were better off and living in Sheldon. This could have been out of habit too as she also suffered for as long as we knew her with gastric tummy problems and ulcers – she took Milk of Magnesia continually for it. I remember visiting her in hospital after she had her gallbladder removed – I think it runs in the family as I had mine removed a few years ago too.

She was so ill that she took time off from cleaning a

church in Solihull, a job she loved doing more than cleaning the buses at the depot down our road. I remember her taking me to the church as a child – she must be a very good person if she was chosen to clean the church, I thought. She was though in all fairness – she was a saintly figure who would always help us out repairing clothes or lending a dish for a cookery lesson. Everyone thought she was our gran and she may as well have been, we loved her just as much.

I loved doing things for her but she only ever wanted to hear about our escapades – whether or not we'd got caught scrumping again, if I was being a good Brownie or not, or one of Dennis's latest scams to raise sixpence. Time is the best thing you can give your loved ones, she would always say. I've always known deep down that this is true. I think we all do really, but we so often tend to forget it as we get caught up in the day-to-day nonsense.

This was brought home to me even more, though, when I arrived one day at her hospital ward a bit later than I would have liked, when she was suffering from one of the gastric complaints that plagued her. The visiting hours were very strict but something told me to get there as soon as I could. I arrived to find the curtains drawn around her bed. I hoped for the best, that perhaps the doctor was in there or she was using the bedpan, but I knew in my heart already. As I pulled back the curtains I saw that all the pain had gone from her face, she looked at peace and young again. But I can still feel the intense grief that struck me as I realised she had definitely gone, and that I'd narrowly missed saying goodbye to her. I became hysterical, so that the nurse had to pull me off as I clung to her. Yet Auntie Lil had also always told us that you never lose someone you've loved – they stay in your heart forever and they are never far away. She was right. I still feel the presence of the loved ones I've lost over the years.

When I think of her now I see her in her dark red burgundy favourite chair by the fire, knitting or sewing, content and smiling. She also had a matching settee with a roly-poly cushion that we weren't allowed to play with.

Auntie Lil had her annoying habits of course, too. She would sleep with her alarm clock under her pillow, which drove me mad as it was ticking away all night. Occasionally, I slept in the same bed as her, if Uncle Ray was home and using the spare room, so I could always hear it. I don't know how or why this quirk developed, but she said she loved the sound of the clock ticking – something about it must have helped lull her off to sleep. I didn't want to upset her but it was keeping me awake all night so eventually I told her, so she put it in the drawer where I couldn't hear it. I've often noticed that this generation shared a trait for keeping items under their pillows, as if by some miracle they'd take them with them, should Heaven come knocking in the night – for Mom it was her purse, every day until she died.

Auntie Lil's house was special for one other reason

too: she had a piano. She treated it as though a precious heirloom. I'm not entirely sure where it came from but it had been there for as long as I could remember. It used to sit there gathering dust and ended up out of tune. I wanted to learn but we never had the time or money. Us kids could do little else but bang on the thing or play 'Can You Wash Your Father's Shirt?', which she once taught us – an old Irish tune from the early twentieth century. I can still remember the lyrics:

> Oh, can you wash your father's shirt?
> Oh, can you wash it clean?
> Can you hang it on the line
> By the village green.

When Lil died, Uncle Ray kept the house exactly the same – they were extremely close and I think he felt any change might have disrespected her memory. In turn Auntie Lil worshipped the ground he walked on – she loved him with an extraordinary fierceness and would constantly sing his praises. I think she felt as though he was the best thing that ever happened to her and seemed to have no regrets about being a single mom.

He was a sweet and gentle man – I think Lil's kindness and love had a profound effect on him. The back-to-backs may have seemed like a different world to him but he was always very polite and genuinely loved spending time with our family. He joined the Army but was still able to come back and visit Lil quite often. I think there were times when he felt concerned about leaving her on her own and I believe he was torn at one point in his life, when he fell in love with a girl whose family were emigrating to Australia – they were both about twenty at the time. He had to make a choice between her and Auntie Lil. Although Lil said he should follow his heart, I think he was scared to leave her alone and thought she'd never fly out to see him. A tough decision but he decided to stay in England. They continued writing to each other for years but he never changed his mind – and he never married. I think there were times he felt lonely, especially after Auntie Lil died. He and my brother Dennis were always particularly close – Ray encouraged Dennis to join the Army and was a positive influence on him.

After Lil died I used to visit Ray and clean and cook for him and he visited us for Christmases in Sheldon once in a while, but it was never quite the same without her. I still miss her so much. I've no idea what happened to the piano either, but I hope it's being played wherever it is.

Auntie Lil was definitely the softest of all Mom's siblings. Uncle Ernie used to be a boxer and still attempted to put those skills to use in more raucous nights down Arthur Street!

Auntie Phoebe was the most outspoken of them all, especially when it came to the topic of my dad. She'd done rather well for herself, marrying a guy with a decent job, and lived in what we would call a terraced town house now, in an upmarket area of Millward Street, just down the road from the wash baths in Green Lane.

She had her own decent-sized front door with a big knocker on the front that led into a room from the street. There was no hallway but it led to a well-furnished front-room living room, with two armchairs and a sideboard with white dogs made out of crockery upon them. Ornaments such as this always jumped out at me – we had nothing like that in our living room at home. Phoebe had her own garden and house with an entry that led round to a spacious garden.

Although I think Auntie Lil at times had her reservations about Dad, she was a lot more diplomatic – in fact, I never heard her speak out of turn about anyone. But Phoebe as the second, perhaps more outspoken elder sister, was far more vocal. She wasn't shy of slating his worst characteristics – she thought he had a selfish streak and didn't help Mom out as much as he could. Often she would say: 'He can't help with housekeeping but he can afford fags and a pint though.' She and Dad were often at loggerheads.

I think some of this anger towards him did stem from jealousy, though. Phoebe's main objection seemed to be that he was always getting Mom pregnant. Rather than congratulate my parents on their next baby, she would say: 'He only 'as to take his trousers off, hang 'em up and you're in the club again!' Her sadness would be underlined with: 'It's not fair, you have too many kids.' She only had one son, Brian, and I know she would have liked more.

To the extent that I know she once asked if she could adopt me. I overheard this and was relieved when the request ended in heated words and Dad, as was his usual response, showed Auntie Phoebe the door. I'm glad he did. As much as she lived in a nicer neighbourhood and home I loved Mom, Dad and my siblings with all my heart and couldn't have imagined life away from them. It warmed me to hear them put their foot down. I know it took Dad quite a long time to speak to Phoebe again after that.

My dad was born in 1924. I never got to know his parents because there was a big family falling-out and he stopped speaking to them. Although I got to know his brothers and sisters throughout my early childhood, my grandparents on Dad's side remained a mystery. But one day at Auntie Lil's house, when I was about seven, I was out in the front garden waiting for my friend, June. I noticed a lady with white hair, neatly tied in a small bun at the back, leaning on the gate, staring at me. She was wearing a white apron over a dark dress. The first thoughts that came to me were: 'I wonder why she looks so sad and old.'

When I went in and told my aunt she was a bit edgy and awkward about it and said, 'Oh, she's just a neighbour.' It unsettled me a little – there was something about the way the woman had stared that left me feeling as though I'd done something wrong. I'd told Auntie Lil that she looked cross with me and that she frightened me. Something about her also looked familiar.

Auntie then said rather hurriedly: 'Oh, er, she's your grandmother, your dad's mom. There was a big family row and we never talk to them.' As was often the way with adults, they'd deliver these statements in a slightly clipped tone that you knew put an end to any further questioning – children should be seen and not heard, as always. But of course I was intrigued and it made sense as to why something about her looked familiar now. Our family have strong genes and are quite sallow in colour – if you see one of us, you would recognise us all.

I was fascinated. Here was my grandma that I never knew, living next door to Auntie Lil, so naturally, I went home asking loads of questions.

My dad wasn't too keen on talking, Dennis and Mom were a little less reticent, but I couldn't get any clear answers. However, a few weeks later, I was making the bus journey with my two elder brothers, Dennis and David, and my younger brother, Alan. I wasn't quite sure why we were suddenly being propelled into this situation but I think we all felt as though we were walking into the lions' den. Why now? What was the secret behind all this? Why had Dad looked so angry? And why had Mom seemed so wary as she waved us off?

Our grandmother's house was warm but it seemed dark and foreboding in there, not as light and airy as Auntie Lil's. There was a strong smell of tobacco that made me cough almost immediately. Then I noticed an old man sitting by the open coal fire, smoking a pipe. I found out afterwards he was our step-grandfather but he never bothered saying much to us – he just coughed and grunted a few times in our direction. I wanted to go straight back to Auntie Lil's house and clung to Dennis's trousers; I was so scared of these strangers.

Grandma shot quite a few questions at us – namely, where we went to church and what school we attended. I just stood there frightened, for once I'd lost my tongue. Dennis took to it though with a confident swagger, as was his way, and did most of the talking. It later turned out he had met them a couple of times before years ago.

Grandma sat us down at the table and put large dinners in front of us – decent slices of meat, plenty of potatoes and vegetables. This in itself was bewildering. I didn't know where to begin – they looked like dinners fit for an ogre. Even Dad was never given a plate that size. Just one alone would have fed the seven of us!

She was staring at us and kept saying, 'Eat up! You look as if you need a good feed, you'll grow up to be big and strong if you eat it all.' But I felt sick with the smell of the pipe that the man was smoking and the amount that was on my plate. I was glad when we went back to Auntie Lil's house and vowed I wouldn't go back. Looking back, I think part of me felt quite judged.

A couple of weeks later I came home from school to find the living-room curtains drawn, making the room even more gloomy than it normally was. My Auntie Lil was there. Dad was also home from work, which I thought was strange. Perplexed, I looked around at the sad faces and said in a loud voice, 'Why are you all sitting in the dark?' My aunt immediately shot back, 'Hush, your grandmother 'as passed away!'

I felt quite sad thinking of the grandmother that I only just met. I wondered how she felt about meeting us all and if she wished she'd broached it sooner. Perhaps she knew she was dying and wanted to offer an olive branch, make a connection or at least see us. I wonder if she'd seen and heard me play in the wild garden at my Auntie Lil's and wished we could have spent more time together.

The row must have been bad not to speak to my entire family. I often thought about her after that large dinner she gave us and regret that I wasn't so chatty and nice to her, but I was only six years old. It seems strange and sad that children often pay for the fallouts of previous generations. Of course we could have made more effort when we saw her, but we were only kids, thrown into a difficult situation. I'd love to go back in time to change that and spend some proper time with her.

I do not know to this day why my dad fell out with his parents, but I remember the grandmother I never got to know. The image of her leaning over the fence looking at me sadly still hasn't left me and I often say a little prayer for her.

3

My Siblings and
an Unconventional
Wartime Birth

All in all, Mom had seven children during our time at
Arthur Street – as Auntie Phoebe would bemoan,
Dad only seemed to look at her and she'd be 'in the
club'. She was an extremely thin woman who never put
on weight, even in her later years when she was eating
better, so the bumps that invariably emerged around her
tummy throughout my childhood seemed all the more
mysterious. We all began to acknowledge what each one
would eventually bring, though – one more mouth to feed
that Mom and Dad couldn't afford.

I know very little of what precautions my parents would
have used – the contraceptive pill was yet to make an
appearance on the market – but Mom seemed so fertile she
was eventually sterilised after her final child, Kevin, who

she had when we'd moved away to the suburb of Sheldon in 1962 or 1963. Who knows how many she would have gone on to have otherwise?

There's rarely a time I remember when she wasn't juggling child-rearing demands under fraught circumstances – whether soothing a suckling baby while chopping carrots or trying to get the fire going with the draw tin. During time-pressured wash days we would often have to leave two babies at a time crying in the pram or free to crawl around in the yard, under the motto that fresh air was good for them.

And as you might expect from nine births, not all of them went according to plan. Mom was to discover the sterling support of Nancy Nee on hand for the first time, on Christmas Day, 1944, when all she thought she had to deal with was sorting the dinner out. She was expecting her second child but it wasn't due until the middle of January so she was getting on with yuletide preparations, making it as merry as it could be during wartime.

Basic foods were scarce so to pull off a roast dinner tested all resources as ever – turkey was unaffordable so it's likely dinner would have been a cut of rabbit meat roasting on the stove – no respite for a pregnant lady then. Presents were discouraged as people were encouraged to contribute to the war effort, but Mom was to receive an unexpected gift that day in the form of a newborn, my brother David – a story that has passed into legendary status in our family.

Dad was on leave from the Navy for Christmas. I doubt

he planned it that way for the birth – as I've said earlier, men generally weren't expected to be present for these events – so he must have got the shock of his life too, and in all honesty would probably rather have missed it!

It was Dennis who instigated Mom's waters prematurely breaking on this occasion. Although it may have been Christmas Day, there was no let up on the domestic chores either – as ever, she was trying to dry sheets and clothes around the coal fire. Dennis, who would have been scarcely more than one, was crawling around the flagstone flooring when he pushed the clothes horse onto the coal fire – Health and Safety would have a field day now. To Mom's horror, the clothes quickly went up in flames, as did one of Dad's homemade rugs. So, as half the room caught light, poor pregnant Mom was caught between stamping out and extinguishing the spreading flames and dealing with the sharp stabbing pains of her imminent labour!

Women left at home had their own battles to fight, right there on their own hearth – if it wasn't Hitler trying to set your front room on fire, it was your own toddler running rampant! Fortunately, through the thin walls the neighbours quickly heard her screams – Ernie and Lily Jeys were over to help subdue the blaze and Nancy Nee was called – as quick as a flash she was there to help Mom give birth there and then in the living room. For years afterwards she joked that it wasn't the only thing to go up in flames – her Christmas dinner was ruined, as was Mom's. All that wasted food – and with a war on, too!

Fortunately, of course, it all ended happily with the birth of David, a beautiful little boy, and Christmas wouldn't have been Christmas each year in our house without this torrid tale being recounted yet again before we sang 'Happy Birthday' to him. Despite arriving during one of the earth's biggest ever conflicts, when the world, as well as the net curtains, were in cinders, he was a miracle – a beautiful bouncing bundle of joy, whose early brush with near disaster set a precedent. Whether he was being run down by a car or getting his fingers stuck in the door or grate above the coal 'ole, where the coal was dropped down, he was the cat with nine lives as our elders would say, narrowly escaping catastrophe at every turn. David had a slew of visitors the day he was born – from Auntie Lil to Ray and Auntie Phoebe, although they were quickly enlisted for the clean-up job rather than given too much time to coo over the new baby.

Dad also had to spend some time in the Brig (prison) as he was late getting back to his ship – no kindly understanding captain or commander back then, encouraging him to spend time with his new son, there was a war on. It was at least another two years until Dennis and David saw their father again. David remembers Dad returning in his sailor suit, walking up the entry to the small fenced-in yard in our courtyard. He bent down and said, 'Hello son, I'm your dad.' Apparently David returned this great declaration with a tirade of screams as he clung to Mom's legs.

David really was at his happiest when covered in bike

oil from taking the chain off his bike to fixing or mending punctures. Out of all the boys, he was probably the quietest though and even a little bit shy – he didn't have the same cheeky outgoing temperament of the others.

For one of his combined birthday and Christmas presents, my parents – driven potty by David unscrewing absolutely anything he could get his hands on – saved up to buy him a Meccano set. He was over the moon and played with it for hours, constructing all kinds of contraptions. Mom looked so happy and proud to see him occupied with his favourite pastime.

I was born at Lordswood Maternity Hospital in March 1946. Dad was particularly pleased – he was proud of his two boys but kept saying, 'We need a girl.' After Mom gave birth to me she took care to follow a postnatal superstition called being 'churched' that many other Brummie mothers adhered to, if their child was born in hospital. (In fact, 'the Churching of Women' is an ancient tradition in the Christian Church, and there is a section in the Book of Common Prayer devoted to it as a rite of thanksgiving.) Mothers wouldn't take their babies out in a pram on the way back from the hospital, or call on anyone, until they'd visited a church to say thank you to Jesus. Mom, having safely delivered her third child and first daughter, dutifully followed this tradition to avoid any bad luck, and to give thanks to God for helping her through the nine months of carrying and a safe delivery. In her case, it was St Aidan's Church in Herbert Road, off Arthur Street, that she carried me into that spring. But with each child, she would just enter the church and kneel down, and if there was a priest on hand, he would bless her and the child (with a home birth, she would go straight to church as soon as she could). I am sure, though, that she was genuinely thankful too, because both my parents had wanted a girl. Although I had little choice but to be a tomboy, scrambling around the bombsites and scrounging for apples, I was a sensitive girl too. When I wasn't chattering away, I often had my head in the clouds, daydreaming, or in a book, although as the oldest daughter in the family, many of the child-rearing and domestic tasks fell to me.

However, we were to be a family mainly dominated by the raucous lads in the brood. You could tell we were all related as we shared very strong physical characteristics – from our dark wavy hair to our piercing, rather mischievous eyes. I think we all had quite a strong Romany look, though I can't see my dad taking to tracing our ancestry – he even had a problem with the Irish! But some of us had more of a twinkle in our eye and were more mischievous than others in our family.

Dennis, as the eldest, had to grow up fast and as we would often hear people say, had 'an old head on young shoulders', aided by Mom's ever-growing brood each year. He was tasked with looking after us kids from as young as eight, when he was only a kid himself. We were his tribe, following him about everywhere under Dad's strict orders to 'look after the kids'. If we hurt ourselves he'd often be the one who got blamed – when our little sister Barbara wanted a go on the bike he would often relent and let her have a go, even though it was too big for her. Of course she'd fall off and hurt herself and then he would take the brunt.

He had the loveliest cheeky grin that won him admirers as early as nine or ten. One of them was Mrs Beighton, who lived at 85 Arthur Street and ran the little grocer's down the road. She was a lovely lady, who helped with our finances substantially because we were able to pay 'on the strap' with her. Each week she would write up what Dad owed her in a big red book and he would pay her at the end of the week, everything from his Woodbines to lard or cheese.

She was certainly the friendliest person who worked there – I missed the like of her when large department stores and supermarkets became more commonplace because she always had time for a chat. A round figure of a woman, she had a bright red face that glistened when she spoke and a cheeky glint of a sparkle in her eyes. She was never without her white apron over a plain dress. A kind and generous woman, she would always treat us – when she cut a piece of cheese, she'd give us an extra sliver to try. As a child, you never knew the full extent of what people were going through but it didn't matter with her – she always seemed to have a cheery disposition. No doubt she suffered her fair share of disappointment and sadness but she somehow left us feeling loved, happy and important. We were never just kids running errands for our mom – she cared about our opinion as well, asking us how something tasted and whether or not it was to our liking. We would wait in turn for her to serve us and let others go before us. But she was definitely at the mercy of Dennis's charms. He'd sidle up to her at the counter, covered in cuts and bruises from his latest adventures out on the bombsite or the yard, his hair and face streaked with dirt, eyes twinkling through wayward masses of unruly dark hair. She'd say, 'You're gonna have the ducks off the water before much longer' (Mom had to translate this one for me) but he had a way with the ladies even then. And ever the entrepreneur with a mind for business, Dennis would use the same trick each week when Dad sent him off to settle the bill – he'd add a halfpenny on so that the rest of us kids could have some sweets. Mrs Beighton knew the score but never told on us and would always put a little extra in our tuck bag. We'd either hide the sweets or eat them on the way back from the moneylender on Kingston Road.

The third boy in our family was Alan, born barely a year after me, in the spring of 1947. Another very good-looking lad, with the signature curly dark hair and cheeky smile, the girls also used to swoon over him, from eight to eighty.

Barbara was three years younger than me, born towards the end of 1949. As was common then, we were dressed exactly the same. I don't think this was any conscious desire to quash our individuality – this was in an age before the dawning of the teenager, so children tended to be dressed as though they were mini versions of their parents. There was very little acknowledgement of individuality, or at the least, it certainly wasn't encouraged. It still amazes me today, the amount of choice children are given, even in deciding what they wear. But I remember how much it used to irritate me that we were always dressed identically. With our long black curly hair and big brown eyes, it was only our difference in ages that meant you could tell us apart.

One Christmas, when I was about seven or eight, I put my foot down: to be different from Barbara, I was determined to have my own blue coat with a velvet trim navy blue collar, just as Princess Anne had worn as a young girl. Mom must have borrowed the money to pay for it, but it was a relief to wear something that meant people could tell me and my sister apart for a change. She was my only other sister though so we were close and I used to mother her quite a lot. We all had an artistic and practical streak that we inherited from our parents. Barbara and I loved making dolls and reading stories about fairies together in the attic – we made paper dolls out of cardboard, then mixed flour and water together in a jam jar to use as glue. Dresses were made out of the backs of wallpaper, then coloured in with my crayons. We never could afford notebooks or drawing books, but Mom would give us leftover scraps that we'd draw on for hours, entertaining ourselves.

Barbara was loving and trusting, with an outgoing nature. Like me, she was something of a chatterbox – she showed affection and a sweet nature to almost everyone she met, even the rent man when he came to our house.

Barely a year later after Barbara, Stephen arrived the following August. As one of the younger boys, he would sleep in the single bed in Mom and Dad's room along with Philip, who was born two years later. They both loved the attention that often comes with being younger and seemed to inherit the cheeky rogue gene so common in our family, as well as the dominant, signature dark curls we all had, yet had a way of talking themselves – always together, they seemed to get out of any trouble they got into as well!

Mom had a bit of a break for the rest of the decade until Josephine was born once we'd moved into our new home in February 1959. By then, memories of the Luftwaffe circling overhead were long gone. We were at the end of a decade where hope and optimism glimmered, not only in the advent of the Swinging Sixties but the luxuries of our new home. Mom was amazed to find that our new accommodation had not one indoor toilet but two, as well as running hot water with a bath. These new mod cons were not to be the only surprise in store that day. She was so overcome with excitement at the mod cons in our new home, her waters broke and she was rushed to Marston Green Hospital, where she gave birth to our baby sister, Josephine, who must have been desperate to join in on all the fun and excitement of our new home.

A beauty with a mass of black curls, it was wonderful to have another girl in the family – she made the total three in all. To celebrate her arrival, we dusted off an old fashioned gramophone left behind in one of the bedrooms. Even by our standards it was pretty passé – you had to put a small needle on the arm of it and wind it up – but we didn't mind. It was wonderful to dance and sing all night in celebration of our new home and our new baby girl, but there was also a sense that the tougher years of the past decade were winding to a close.

A gorgeous little girl, I felt as though I was Josephine's aunt rather than her sister in some ways as there was a 13-year age gap between us – by the time I'd left home and got married at twenty-one, she was still only eight. It was the same with Kevin, the last to be born in 1963, which means that Mom had children across three decades in all! He was the baby of the family or the 'scrapings of the pot' as we used to say. Another beautiful child, he was as good as gold and grew up fast with us lot showing him the ropes. He was quick to learn because of this and like Dad, was very good at woodwork and building – he could turn his hand to any job around the house or garden. Kevin was only four when I married Ray. Because he was so much younger he was like a brother to my two young children as well when they came along, rather than an uncle figure.

Child Benefit payments weren't brought in until the late seventies so many mothers, Mom included, retained a 'make do and mend' mentality from the war. Mom was fortunate that Auntie Lil was always happy to help out with our clothes – I think she could have carved out an incredible career as a dressmaker or designer, had she had the opportunity as a young woman, but she had the pressure of bringing up Ray and Mom to juggle with her cleaning work. Often I wonder what Mom would have done with her life too if she hadn't had the pressure of raising us all. I used to see her face light up whenever she arranged bluebells in a jam jar to add some colour and life to our living room. She never missed an opportunity to arrange flowers and had a similar eye for design as Dad. It wasn't much of a surprise to learn as I grew up that as a young woman she'd wanted to be a florist.

If money was no object she would have accepted the job that a local florist offered her. But the pay was so low her family advised against it, especially as she was about to marry – she was able to earn a lot more in a factory. However, I saw her come into her own when we moved away and she had her own garden to play with – she kept it beautifully and grew vegetables and flowers of all varieties. She also kept a garden when my parents bought a caravan in Ludlow, which brought her much joy. My sister Barbara shared Mom's passion for flowers and went on to become a florist after she left school.

4

Clip Round the Ear 'Oles and School Discipline

Domestic tasks dominated the majority of Mom's time. Therefore, family meals were kept to a fairly regimented structure in the Rainbird household, which was fairly usual for other families in our neighbourhood. Without fail, at 5.30 Mom would always have the table set before she headed off to work at the sausage factory Bywaters, down Coventry Road, where she packed meat from 6–10pm. Other than that though, our meals were very basic. In the early fifties we were still in the aftermath of rationing so the choice was limited and there was not much variation from evening to evening, not that we knew any different then. The system hadn't altered much since the war. Each person had a ration book. They contained tokens that could be saved up or used whenever the owner wished. The shopkeeper would then remove these tokens before handing out the items. Most adults had a buff coloured ration book, while children aged between five and sixteen had a blue one. Mom would have received fruit, milk and eggs.

Our meal portions were meagre and consisted of mashed potatoes, cabbage boiled within an inch of its life and rabbit stew. Other regular meals included sausage or corn beef with mash. Liver and onions were an occasional treat – Mom would buy meat from the butcher on Coventry Road – as were salmon and shrimp paste sandwiches. Chips and egg have always been a standard favourite of me and Ray, but we never had them back then. Another occasional treat was dried bread, which we'd toast in front of the fire on a fork. If we had enough sugar to go round, we'd sprinkle a little over the top before we folded and ate it – delicious!

People turn their noses up at spam now but it was a versatile little meat that almost everyone had after the war on ration – we fried it with potatoes and cabbage or ate it from the tin cold or in a sandwich or salad. I never ate it after I left home because I hated the taste but in those days we had to eat up or go hungry.

If we had any cocoa, which was very rare, we'd mix it together with sugar and drop it into a cone-like piece of paper – it tasted a little like chocolate kali or sherbet. We loved sweets from the shop when we could get them but soon became expert at creating our own alternative versions.

In the mid-fifties Mom started shopping at the Co-op down Coventry Road. Us kids always loved the familiarity of the smaller shops and getting food 'on the strap' from our favourite Mrs Beighton. To me, the relatively large size of the Co-op made it seem a lot more impersonal, although in those days the assistant still served customers from behind the counter as all the groceries were stocked up on shelves behind them. It would take a long time for the assistant to pack items together, from sugar to margarine and bread. The process was made even longer because of the chutes that would send your money up to an office above, where the change would be worked out and sent back down again. Mom preferred the Co-op though because the food was cheaper than the local stores and she collected points in her dividend book. I can still remember our dividend number all these years later – 29 15 60. At the end of the year you would receive cash to spend on extra treats – for example, broken biscuits. No plastic bag waste then, though – we carried all our items in a brown paper bag.

Once rationing ended, food didn't suddenly become any more exciting because we were so financially stretched. (De-rationing in the UK had begun in 1948, but food rationing didn't finally end until July 1954.) Most evenings we were all going to bed with rumbling tummies and around the age of ten I was diagnosed as anaemic because I hadn't been getting enough meat. Interestingly though, I would say my health is incredibly good at the age of seventy-one

– I'm strong and I seem to have more energy than younger people, so I think a menial diet early on had its blessings to some degree.

Although food was scarce, as a baby boomer our generation benefitted from continuing improvements to the welfare system too, set in motion as early as 1918 when the Maternity and Child Welfare Act was passed. This gave local authorities power to appoint medical officers of health and health visitors and to establish clinics and welfare centres that provided free and cheap milk and cod liver oil.

During World War II children and expectant mothers were advised to take cod-liver oil and drink orange juice throughout wartime rationing. This continued after the war to boost their intake of vitamins and prevent diseases. Back then we would queue for hours at the welfare centre on Coventry Road to receive our free portions, but once inside we didn't mind sitting around as it was warm and there were toys and other children to play with; we were treated kindly by the nurses and Mom would talk to the other mothers. I don't think any child enjoyed their dose of cod-liver oil, but the lovely taste of orange juice helped wash it down. Mom also received free powdered baby milk and we drank sterilised milk because in our house fresh milk would have gone off very quickly without a fridge. For this reason we never bought butter either – lard was part of our staple diet. Mom would buy it from Mrs Beighton and keep it in the scullery, the coolest place in the house. Meals were always ready in time for Dad, which gave him enough time to have a 'quick swill' under the cold tap before he headed off to visit the Prince Albert pub on our street.

Whether Dad did or didn't go to the pub was never up for discussion and I certainly never heard Mom question him on this. He did work extremely hard as the main breadwinner, taking on many extra jobs besides his shop steward work at the Morris Minor car factory at Drews Lane – from chimney sweeping to woodwork – so in some ways I think he deserved his relaxation time with his other friends, who were all leaving their wives at home or at work too. However, when I hear stories now of dads reading their children bedtime stories it comes home to me again what different times we're living in. Back then, the topic of dads playing a more active role in parenting was never even remotely touched upon. But I don't feel resentment towards my parents for this either. There were so many restrictions on the amount of time and love that they could give. Hugs, cuddles and kisses were few and far between in our household – there were seven mouths to feed and attend to and I think that just as our food was rationed, there was only so much love and attention to go round too. It's interesting to reflect on this though because I think these experiences have influenced my own parenting style over the years. I truly believe that time is one of the greatest gifts you can give your children and it's more important than money – if they feel loved, wanted and as though they belong, they will go out into the world with this knowledge and wear it almost like armour.

Auntie Lil wasn't overenthusiastic with hugs or kisses either but I do remember her visiting our house in Sheldon, where we moved after the back-to-backs, not long before she died. I was distracted with cleaning the cooker and vacuuming – the cleaning ethic instilled in me from a young age by Mom, who kept our floors spotless. Auntie Lil patted the sofa and said to me: 'The dirt and muck will still be here when I'm dead, come and talk to me.' She was right, and I always remember her saying this to me whenever I get caught up with trivial details or matters. However, I do think parents were too disciplined back then too. People who grew up in the fifties have a tendency to look back at the decade as a simpler, less complicated time when children respected their elders and to a large extent behaved better. They didn't speak out of line in either the classroom or at home and lived by the most ancient of Victorian mantras: children should be seen and not heard. But I think much of this 'good behaviour' was instilled through fear. In my opinion there was far too much knee-jerk discipline meted out in our home and at school. And invariably this came in the form of the 'clip round the ear 'ole', a term you rarely hear these days. It wasn't uncommon to receive one from the local bobby either – imagine the trouble a police officer would get into now for taking a child's discipline into his own hands! My grandson often looks baffled when I talk about it because he can't quite believe it was such a common occurrence. And indeed, it has long dissolved into history, another ghostly relic of the past, along with the demolished back-to-backs. For our generation, most kids were braced for the clip round the ear 'ole and our household was no different.

I remember once when Dad came home from the pub one night with the usual crowd. I couldn't sleep because it was winter and I was absolutely freezing. As usual, I was top and tailing with the boys and there were feet, arms and legs everywhere you moved. The boys had pulled the blankets off me and I had no share of the covers. So I made my way downstairs to ask Mom and Dad for an overcoat – it was common for us to use these on the bed if it was cold, because there weren't any spare blankets.

I can still remember the look on my dad's face as he went red. 'What do you mean, an overcoat? They are called blankets!' he shouted. He gave me one of his looks as if to say 'Just you wait!' Obviously, I realise now that he was ashamed we used overcoats as blankets and was too embarrassed to admit this in front of his friends. He told me to get back up to bed and that Mom would bring me up the spare blanket, not before giving me a quick clip round the old ear 'ole. Kids, eh? Their most innocent comments often have a way of showing up adults.

Later, Mom crept up with Dad's gabardine overcoat. The fabric was an extremely heavy material but provided a much-needed extra layer of warmth. By that point I was too wide awake to settle down anyway but it wasn't until years later that I understood how humiliating this must have been for him. In fact, it was a memory that returned when I visited the restored back-to-backs as there was a bed with a coat just the same, strewn across the top.

The majority of the clip round the ear 'oles came from Dad – most offences were caused by interrupting *The Archers* or talking while the news was on the wireless. As the eldest, Dennis was often expected to 'set an example' and tended to bear the brunt of Dad's temper. However, Mom wasn't above dishing out the odd painful clip too. I still remember how much they could sting as her fingers were particularly thin and bony – a lefthander from her could leave us reeling. She would, however, plead with Dad not to hit us round the head – sometimes we got three or four smacks, or what you'd call a clout. But if we so much as looked as though we were about to cry, we'd be told: 'Shut your crying, I'll give you something to cry about!' This was normally prompted by a smack and then we really would be crying.

Interestingly though, Mom was often the first to stick up for us, especially when she felt we'd been mistreated by the teachers at my infant and junior school. Built in 1879, Dixon Road was one of the earliest schools to be built in Small Heath to cope with the rapidly expanding population. A large, imposing red brick structure, with some of the Gothic features so synonymous with Victorian architecture, to me it seemed enormous. It was only a short ten-minute walk from Arthur Street so I would set off with my brothers and my sister Barbara each morning.

I have some very happy memories of my time there. I hated learning to sew but loved art, reading and singing hymns in assembly. I particularly enjoyed the teachers reading stories to us. One of my fondest memories is being given the responsibility of ringing the bell at playtime – I thought I was the absolute bee's knees, lifting up that heavy brass structure to let everyone know playtime was over. In many ways I was oblivious to the stresses and strains of being a poor kid from the back-to-backs and as carefree and happy as any of the other more well off kids who lived down Coventry Road. Like the yard, the playground was a great leveller and any class war divisions melted away over a game of Skip Rope, Hopscotch or Kiss Chase. And of course, all of us received the same bottle of free milk every day, which I loved because of the fresher taste.

Kids are quick to pick up on differences though and these were probably made the most apparent during meal times, one time of the day when some conflict would arise. There was no escaping the fact if you were a free school meals kid back then – there was very little discretion as you carried your green ticket with 'F' in large print up to the cashier. The kids who could afford it had buff-coloured tickets. It actually didn't bother me at all – for a start you got a lot more food on your plate as a free school meals kid, but we hated the kids who would taunt us about it, saying things like 'Oh, here come the green cards'. I really appreciated that meal of the day – over the decades school dinners have rarely been renowned for their gourmet delights but we received decent portions of potatoes and meat pie.

And yes, we had to behave ourselves in class. We sat at singular wooden desks in rows – we had to keep our backs as straight as possible as we stared ahead at the blackboard.

I've realised since delving back into the past that it's only now that certain memories are bubbling to the surface, several I think I'd blocked out. Although I was generally very happy at school, I think there were some teachers who relished the days when corporal punishment was still legal just a little too much. The preferred tools were the ruler and cane, although a couple of them weren't averse to throwing the odd blackboard rubber either – the aim that some had being quite incredible! The cane seemed to be used for really naughty behaviour while the ruler was kept for the not so naughty behaviour, but in hindsight I think the cane was reserved for the boys instead, perhaps because they assumed they could 'take it' more. I never got the cane, but Dennis did a couple of times. He had a very vivid imagination that could get him into trouble, always making up stories. I remember being hit with a ruler just the once and I still can't really remember what I'd done to deserve it. I hated the teacher who did it, but I still have problems picturing his face. I just remember how he made me feel – humiliated in front of the other children.

I was often in trouble because I had to stay off school on a Monday for wash day so I don't think the teachers were too sympathetic towards me to start with. A letter was sent to Mom about my absences, and when I was asked about them I replied that I was unwell and had a note from my mother. And I was known for my non-stop chatter. I often got bored during prayers in assembly and started nattering away to Ann and Valerie. This aspect of my personality irritated my parents as well as the teachers, and I was punished by being made to write out 'I must not talk in class' one hundred times. However, Mom was furious to see the red welted marks inflicted on my legs from the ruler and Dennis's hands by this particular teacher – 'I can't believe that!' she exclaimed. 'What did you to deserve that?' She grabbed both me and Dennis by the arm, muttering, 'My kids aren't that naughty,' and marched us down to the school and shouted at the teacher as all the children were filing out. Although I was shocked and perhaps a little mortified, what she said has always stayed with me: 'The world will knock my kids about so you don't need to.' The teacher went red and stuttered: 'If children deserve it, that's what we do.'

'Not to my kids you won't!' Mom responded. 'Do not *ever* touch them again.'

The teacher went quiet and was obviously shocked she had the nerve to confront him. And perhaps he even felt a little humiliated because really, I don't think we'd done anything to warrant these punishments. But he never touched me or any of my brothers ever again. Mom was firm with us but I'm touched that she always stuck up for us too. And she was right about one thing: I definitely received some severe 'knocks' in life, as she put it, many of us have, but I don't believe school should be the place to receive your first experience of them.

With Mom out at work packing sausages at the Bywaters factory in Coventry Road, and Dad's evening sojourns to the pub, Dennis was often left in charge of us kids. Today, the majority of parents wouldn't dream of leaving their son, who's no more than seven or eight, in charge of four other young children. In fact, it is, of course, illegal. But 'Health and Safety' regulations were still light years away – from the age of five I was picking up scorching irons with rags off the range and Dad wouldn't think twice about leaving his matches around for us to pick up and play with. So the question of whether or not Dennis was responsible enough to look after us all was never even taken into account, it was just a given and I'm certain it was never discussed.

I loved my older brother dearly, and most of the time he did a very good job of minding us. Still, there were times when I think the power of being left in charge of us went to his head a little. Not least because Dad could be really tough on him and I think there were times when he needed to assert his control. One evening though, just before Bonfire Night, Dennis was looking after us kids and enjoying every minute of it. He was sat in Dad's favourite chair, watching TV and warming his feet in front of the fire when he asked me to make him a cup of tea. He told me he'd let me stay up a little longer – we were all due to go to bed by about ten – if I did. So I heated up the water on the range and made him a pot of tea.

Once I'd carried the cup of tea over to him he looked at me, pulled an expression and said, 'Ha, ha! You can't really, you have got to go to bed now. Off you go!' Then he told me I was too young to watch the programme anyway. It was only something like *Dixon of Dock Green*. My brother was always cheeky and normally I didn't mind his teasing but it made my blood boil the way he'd moved the goalposts and I was fed up with him laying down the ground rules every time he looked after us. I screamed back: 'Dennis, you ain't the boss, you ain't our dad!' as I threw the hot cup of tea over him. Then it was his turn to explode. He picked up the teapot, chucked the lid off and threw tea over me, scalding my chest. It would have been sitting on the range for about half an hour so was extremely hot.

I screamed the place down and Dennis looked terrified when he realised what he'd done. In a panic, he fetched Mrs Nee – the voice of all reason and resident doctor, as well as midwife. She looked at my burns and instantly told him to run up to the factory and fetch Mom. He must have been quaking in his boots as we went up there to tell her, knowing she'd be furious at him not only hurting me but for interrupting her shift too – it's unlikely she would have been paid for the hours she missed.

There's always a certain initial victory in squabbles

between brothers and sisters when one of them realises just how deeply they'll be in trouble. 'He burnt me, he burnt me!' I squealed, actually in genuine pain, as my parents came home, their faces both as red as thunder. But my triumphant feelings were quickly quashed as Dad ripped his belt off and strapped Dennis – something that was a rare occasion indeed but quite terrifying to witness. He then shouted at him to get up the stairs to bed.

I stood there whimpering in quite a sorry state. Tea leaves were stuck to my chest, which made it look and feel worse. The fluid had also dripped down to my feet so they were scalded with blisters appearing on them. (I don't recall being taken to the doctor's, though, and I have no long-term scarring, so I must have healed quickly.) The next day I was sore and blistered as I woke and I wasn't looking forward to Bonfire Night. I have to say though, I did milk it a little because Mom and Dad seemed genuinely concerned and were being quite tender towards me, which was quite a new experience. Dennis was still in the doghouse of course and looked contrite for a change, the cheeky smile wiped off his face. Of course his gentle behaviour towards me wasn't to last that long and he was soon out and about on Bonfire Night, causing mischief once again.

As I was on my way down our entry to call on Ann and Valerie, trying to dodge all the kids having fun running up and down it, Dennis threw a jumping jack firework up the entry. It made me jump up at what felt like a couple of feet in the air – the shock of which made some of my blisters burst. He seemed genuinely sorry when he realised what he'd done and promised he hadn't seen me down there. I decided to believe him because I'm pretty sure he was telling the truth. I also hated the thought of him getting into more trouble so I never told our parents. Thankfully, the evenings were a lot calmer than this most of the time and we all rubbed along pleasantly enough. In the summer we would play out till ten but if it was colder weather, I tended to sit in the attic and make my own dolls. Although we wound each other up on occasion, ultimately we were protective of each other too.

Every Saturday evening Dad would take Mom out to the Prince Arthur pub down our road. This was their chance to both get a little dressed up, though this was certainly not one of Small Heath's most glamorous venues. Dad would normally only let me hang around outside unless he sent me there to fetch a jug of ale when he fancied a night in with his feet up in front of the TV. 'Don't spill any!' he'd order. This was of course in the days when children could still buy alcohol. If I was lucky, I might get a packet of crisps as a thank you.

I hated the smell of stale booze and fags in there, as well as the tail end of a fight I might catch in a haze of smoke. In between some punch-up over a deal gone wrong on the black market – Dad would often procure a bottle of whisky or a chicken for Christmas from there – there'd be the odd sing-song round a piano in the corner to lighten everyone's spirits. Dad would wear a suit while Mom would change from her usual baggy smocks and loose top into a dress. Her special trick was curling her hair using the hot poker – it's a wonder she had any hair left in her later years after what she put it through – and she'd dab just enough red rouge and lippy to lift her dark curls and sparkling brown eyes. She didn't need much make-up though, Mom – she was a real stunner.

This was Dad's way of treating Mom although looking back, I think pub money took precedence over housekeeping money – she was often asking him for more. It was rare to see groups of women in any pub in those days, other than a Saturday night – once they got together though they'd often talk about how skint they were, something the men were normally too proud to discuss. It wasn't necessarily a place for flirting either, as most of the couples down there were married – woe betide any man who looked at Mom anyway!

Spirits were often quite high by the time Mom and Dad arrived back at ours – 3/84 was always the place to return because Mom made cracking cheese and onion sarnies. Ridiculous really, she scrimped and saved to feed us but still couldn't say no to a mob of friends and relatives demanding a good feed at the end of the night. I think she often went without actually and this continued even in our 'wealthier' days when we moved away. I know there were occasions when she skipped meals to make sure one of our boyfriends or girlfriends had enough too.

They would sometimes bring back a large enamel jug of beer to share or Dad would open a bottle of whisky and indulge in one of his favourite pastimes: singing. We always wanted to go and join in – we'd heard 'My Old Man's a Dustman' enough times by now to know all the words and we loved 'Danny Boy'. But this was just before the merriment would often turn sour. It was normally precipitated by Uncle Ernie, who'd been a boxer in his younger days and wanted to prove he still 'ad it. If he wanted to prove it to my dad or Mickey Nee, the night could end on a combustive note. Mom and Nancy would scream for them to 'pack it in', especially when Mom saw one of them reach for a nearby household item to do damage with – often it was one of Dad's own stools he'd made that ended up over Ernie's head, and thankfully not the draw tin, which could potentially kill a man.

Often we'd get out of bed and sit on the stairs to listen to the commotion downstairs. Dad would sometimes catch us and shout up the classic Brummie command: 'Get up the dancers!' (up the stairs) – 'I've told you once, don't let me have to tell you again!' That was normally followed by Mom's favourite expression: 'Doubt the light! We ain't got money to burn!' She meant 'douse' of course, as in to douse a campfire or candle after you've finished with it. For years though, I thought the correct term was 'doubt' – no idea why she swapped a 't' for 's' in this way. Occasionally we'd avoid a bollocking, insisting we were just using the bucket on the landing because 'The po's full, Dad!'

The next day Dad would be hammering away, repairing the broken stool along with his friendships – although even when they'd made up we could guarantee it would happen all over again the following Saturday!

5

The Club and Rent Man, Meddling Nuns and Dodging the School Board

We may well have joked about Mom having OCD today, such was the energy she ploughed into keeping the house clean. Water could be pouring into the attic bedroom from a hole in the roof, or the ceiling might be red with the residue of a recently squashed bug, but the flagstone flooring was kept so sparkly and clean, you could eat your dinner off it.

Mom's secret weapon was ruthless application of red cardinal polish, bought from the Co-op. She showed no mercy when it came to our floor or front step. Whatever the weather, both were scrubbed within an inch of their lives to the extent that much of the step began to wear away over the years. This created a rather slippery dip in the middle, not helped by water from the drains and people's footsteps. Cardinal polish was another common smell in our neighbourhood as many women used it – God knows what chemicals were in it, but I grew to love it, not least because it masked the strong smell of damp. But it's another one that my husband Ray still remembers with a grimace.

I think it was important to Mom because with both her and her husband just about keeping their heads above water, this was one way that she could still hold her head up high. Our house was our haven and she did everything she could to keep it as homely as possible. We might have been living in the slums but by hook and crook, she would make sure that whoever stepped over our hearth, friend or foe, could not find fault with her cleanliness. Because admittedly, over the years there were certainly a few folk more welcome than others. As one of the houses that faced inwards to the court we didn't have a front door, so it was rare that any of our neighbours knocked. A sharp rap at the door normally indicated a visitor from outside of our community. And that normally meant one unavoidable fact: someone wanted paying who we couldn't pay. Mom would literally drop everything – her shovel, poker or draw tin – and make a run for the scullery to hide behind the door before whispering to me in hushed and urgent tones: 'Tell him, "She ain't in, come back next week".' Invariably, this would happen on a Monday. For us, it meant wash day and a visit from the dreaded rent man.

Life is full of contradictions, and often these appear no

more starkly than in childhood. Every week I attended Sunday school at St Aidan's (now All Saints) with my siblings – in all honesty, I think my parents' main motivation for sending us there was to have a break rather than instil in us any good Christian virtues, and it allowed Mom to get the cooking and cleaning done; besides, Sunday school was very much a normal part of life in those days. We didn't mind. Plus, we were always assured of getting a biscuit or two whenever we were there.

But here, the importance of right and wrong was drilled into us. This stuck with me every time I opened the door and lied to the rent man. And it was even worse because he knew I was lying – it was obvious from my guilty expression, bright red face and stammering tiny voice as I avoided any eye contact with him. I knew very little about this thin and small man, probably in his fifties or sixties, with hardly any hair. On a personal level, we didn't even know his name – he was just the 'rent man'. But he scared me to death, with his thin pointed nose and his rent book tightly clutched under the arm of his gabardine Mac.

To be fair, I think he understood the difficult position I was in – not an uncommon one for him to encounter, I'm sure. Most of all, I just remember how bad it left me feeling; I hated lying and realised even at the time that he was just doing his job. In later years though, I've felt less kindly towards him. Of course I never really understood the system we were at the mercy of in those back-to-backs but I realise now that the rent was extortionately high for what we had and many people would have struggled to pay it. This seems particularly unfair when you consider the squalor we lived in and the fact there were rarely any repairs or improvements made to the properties.

From the mid-fifties there was some effort on the council's behalf to raise the standard – we had a small fence put in ('palings' as we called them) to create a tiny garden area in our court that would provide a little extra privacy, which Dad often used for woodwork. But the majority of the time we were living in conditions that were no different to the earlier years of the Victorian era, where the landowner's main focus was squeezing as much profit as possible from substandard housing – these houses were never built to last and we were still bearing the brunt of decisions made all those years ago.

The fear of eviction was always hanging over my parents' heads. I never really understood this at the time and of course it was never discussed in front of us kids, but we knew instinctively on some level that it was a potential threat – not least from our involvement in so many of the scams or measures employed to raise or save money. Mom never had much time to gossip but I once overheard her telling Auntie Lil that a woman up the street had got badly into debt and done a 'moonlit flit' (a runner) before she was evicted. I never really quite understood what they were talking about – they always spoke in hushed tones if I was in earshot or did their best to sweep it under the carpet. In many ways, Mom did her best to keep us as innocent as possible. It was also not uncommon to see people who had been evicted return to sleep in the entry or toilet at night. I have vague memories of seeing a woman with a pram stuffed full of her worldly possessions and a young child at her feet.

Another regular visitor on a Monday was Mr Scott, the club man. This is a job title that has all but died out as far as I know, although he would perhaps be classed as a 'salesman' now. Most of the time he was fairly welcome – as long as he could be paid for any outstanding bills. He pedalled his various wares, from fabrics to curtains, but Mom tended to only ever order sheets from him, which he would bring the following week. He was in his forties and looking back, I think he might have had a bit of a drink problem – his face was red, with purple veins and rosacea. But to me he seemed 'posher' than us. 'Posh' to us meant anyone who had nice shoes. By 'nice shoes' I mean shoes that were black, patent and not held together by cardboard in their soles. It was anyone who lived in a house with a toilet inside, went to C&A for new clothes instead of cast-offs from the market and talked a little 'less Brummie' than us. But his 'poshness' was also reflected in his manner towards us – he acted as though we were a little beneath him. He never waited for a response when he asked if he could come in – his foot was already across the door and he would head for Dad's chair and make himself comfortable before looking at Mom expectantly for a cup of tea. I liked him enough, but I think he took advantage a little and ultimately his main aim was to get us further into debt. Like all of us, I suppose he was just trying to make a living. Of course, he would try to tempt us with his salesman patter, but Mom was rarely swayed. Although she eventually got into debt, she was never one for extravagances and would only buy what she absolutely needed from him.

Occasionally he would charm her into buying an extra set of pillows, which would be added to next week's bill. Whether she was able to pay it back or not was another matter. There were still the odd occasions when I had to lie to him too – paying the rent was the priority so he'd have to wait another week once Mom had found the money from somewhere else – robbing Peter to pay Paul was the way our lives played out. Often, interest was added to the bill if it wasn't paid one week and this added up over the year. Despite this, Mom's mantra was always 'If you can't afford it, you can't have it' and this is one lesson that's stuck with me over the years, not least because I saw how my parents struggled. As hard as Mom and Dad could be, I did respect those values and learnt from them. To this day, Ray and I have always steered clear of debt and we don't even have a credit card.

Later though, when we moved to Sheldon and were a little better off, Mom even ordered candlewick bedspreads from the local club man – a luxurious treat we would never have indulged in, back at Arthur Street.

As if dodging the financial demands of the rent and club

men weren't enough there was one other figure to hide from: the school board man. As with many girls on my street and across the slums, the majority took Monday off. This wasn't out of laziness, I can tell you, simply because it was wash day. Normally, Mom pretended I was ill, but obviously this didn't wash after a while (no pun intended). The school were aware this was a common situation so warning letters were routinely sent out to parents. When these were ignored the school board man would visit our house to complain and tell Mom that if she kept me off school without a good reason she could be fined or even sent to prison. He was a nasty-looking thin man and no fool and he wrote my name down in his book while I hid behind the scullery door. But it wasn't Mom's fault – wash day was a huge job that she couldn't do alone. Today though, the practice of keeping girls back from their education to help with chores would be seen by most people as incredibly unfair and sexist. I didn't mind it at the time – Monday meant sewing, which was my most hated subject. To this day, I refuse to sew on a button so at least I rejected one stereotypically female chore!

Yes, we were blessed with an array of visitors at Arthur Street but perhaps the most interfering and unwelcome of them all were, interestingly, a group of nuns from the Catholic church my dad was raised in. They always arrived unannounced and would step over the threshold as though it was their God-given right.

We weren't raised as Catholics but attended the C of E

church St Aidan every Sunday. Mom and Dad never went – I think Christmas or Easter was the odd exception, as long as Dad's suit wasn't languishing in the pawn shop at the time, of course. But the nuns took it upon themselves to try and tempt Dad back to Catholicism. Admittedly, three Hail Marys was never a phrase you were likely to hear him exclaiming. But the simple fact was that rather than actively avoiding church, my parents just didn't have the time to attend. Ideally, they would have benefitted from some practical or financial help rather than the occasional bit of God bothering, but at least a trip to church each week meant a drink of juice and a biscuit for us kids. I'm sure they knew times were hard for us but having said that, my parents ate sparsely themselves – there were no chicken shops back then and it was unusual to ever see an overweight person.

6

Down the Coal 'Ole,
Queuing for Coal and a Fancy
New Tiled Grate

'**B**lack as coal' is an expression you don't really hear any more. Nowadays, we're fairly far removed from that hard bit of rock and its potent fumes, with our centrally heated houses and gas appliances. But for us growing up in the back-to-backs it was a substance that was absolutely essential for our survival. And as far as that expression went, there was nothing metaphorical about it at all. We knew exactly what it meant. When we looked down at our feet after coming up from the cellar or as was its more appropriate name, the coal 'ole, they were literally black from the coal we'd been walking in. It was the single most important raw material we needed, and whether or not we could obtain it consumed the vast majority of our days. We depended on it for everything – our fires to stay warm, getting our clothes clean, bath night and making sure we ate each day.

During the war the coal ration was set at two and a half tons per household per year, even though the UK was a coal producing country. But this rationing continued up until the fifties too so we were always aware how precious it was, almost like gold dust. We realised this from a young age. Our mom was ever waiting, as were all other housewives in the neighbourhood, for the sound of the coalman's horse trotting slowly by – 'Quick, quick! Go and see if he's dropped 'owt!'

At one point our street was nicknamed Horse Street because this was such a regular sight. It was always a rather droopy, sad and dishevelled-looking horse, no surprise really when you consider the weight it was carrying, but I really felt for the coalman who came hobbling by with his sack – he'd often be carrying as much as a hundredweight of coal (around 112 pounds). It must have been backbreaking work as he heaved it over his shoulder. And even when the coalman had the horses to help him, he still had to heave it up to our entry and into the yard, going back and forth to collect more sacks.

We would always run out to check and see if he'd dropped any coal but more often than not, we'd return empty-handed. It was very rare that these coalmen dropped any in the entry – they were as vigilant as us and knew how precious it was. Occasionally too you might get the odd one who would try to undercut you so it was important you really understood your weights and knew what you were receiving. The value of coal was almost reiterated in the fact that there were no 'IOUs' for its purchase – it was an upfront payment so if you didn't have the cash, you didn't receive it. So Mom and Dad always made sure they had enough money for this particular caller – there were no hiding behind the scullery door antics. If we all had to plan so far ahead in this way now, I imagine we'd think twice before sticking the central heating on!

Once Mom had paid him, the coalman would open up the black grate outside our home, directly above our coal 'ole, which was about two by two feet across. My brother David was constantly getting his fingers stuck in it, such was his curiosity for picking almost everything apart to see how it worked. The coalman would give a quick holler down the hole to check that no one was in there, if you were lucky, before he began to unload it – a hundredweight of coal tumbling into the cellar beneath. It lasted our family around two weeks at the cost of five shillings (25p, but more than £5 in today's money), although obviously, as a large family we had to stretch this as far as possible. I'll never forget the kindness of our neighbours, though. Even some of the more elderly ones such as Mrs Griffin, who would have suffered more in the freezing cold winters, were prepared to be generous, offering their last few pieces of coal if we'd run out.

It was the children's job to go down to the cellar and fetch the coal, a task that we would take in turns. Not surprisingly, none of us relished going down into that dark pit. It was rare we'd have a candle or torch with us either as this meant we'd have one less hand free, so we relied on the little bit of light that fell through the grate occasionally. And because the floors were so filthy down there we didn't wear shoes either, which is why they turned as black as they did. It was quite normal for us to run around with no shoes or socks on in the house anyway as so many of our things had to be kept as pristine as possible for our Sunday best. Needless to say, I absolutely adore my collection of slippers that keep my feet warm now.

From as early as five I remember how frightening it was to venture down those thin concrete steps from the top of the cellar – I hated it. We were sometimes sent down to fetch wood from there too: another essential that had to be kept as dry as possible, this was the best place to keep it warm. I crept down as carefully as I could, feeling my way for anything that could be a mouse or spider, desperate not to feel anything furry run across my feet – I was terrified at the thought of a mouse nibbling at my toes! The cellar was also home to hundreds of beetles, which we used to call 'black bats'.

Other times I'd brace myself for a prank from one of my brothers – Dennis (or rather 'Dennis the Menace' as we called him) was fond of hiding down there and waiting for me to get to the bottom before he leapt out. I would carry the galvanised bucket down, which was already heavy, but I knew it would be worse on the way up once I'd started filling it. Sometimes I would have to make at least three or four trips depending on how much Mom wanted – it was a lot to carry and I couldn't manage it all in one go. Occasionally I would fall down or up the stairs and bruise my legs or knees. This was normally met with a 'What you doing down there?' from Mom or Dad – no time for hugs or kissing it better. I realise some people would say we were 'brought up rough' but we just learnt to get on with the job in hand as we didn't know any different. And there was no point moaning anyway as it would be met with one of those good old clips round the ear 'ole and the threat of really giving you something to cry about. Although those experiences have made me a lot more attentive to my grandchildren and great grandchildren, I appreciate Mom was also under a lot of strain – it was tough for her too and I realise any short-temperedness was a result of sheer exhaustion. We weren't a huggy or kissy family, although I think this was quite the norm for both our culture and our generation.

In later years, when we were a bit older, we went to Herbert Street – not far from Arthur Street – to collect our own coal. This meant it was cheaper for our parents because they cut out the middleman as it was collected directly. But it wasn't so great for us because inevitably, the task fell upon us. In any weather, come rain or shine, Dennis, David, Alan and I would make the trip on a Saturday, where we'd wait in the queue at the coal house – its wooden doors opened at 8am and we aimed to get there as early as possible to avoid waiting too long. Sometimes we all went, including Barbara, to get her out from under Mom's feet, although she would want to come with us anyway.

It was obvious that there were times when it had been broken into overnight – people were that desperate for coal. We had no horse or cart unfortunately so would take the next best thing – the children's pram, a trusty vehicle used for many different purposes. Not only did it serve up to seven children in its time, it bore a particularly heavy load – that of a hundredweight of coal. We normally weren't able to get that much in the pram in one go, it was just too heavy, so we'd have to make several trips and queue up again. Because our need for coal was greater in the winter we were forced to withstand some less than desirable temperatures. It was on these occasions that one of Auntie Lil's knitted balaclavas came in very handy. As for the poor pram, it was sturdy but obviously balked under the strain of this alternative use, once the coalman heaved it on. Sometimes one of the wheels would come off and the four of us would push it home on three wheels if we couldn't fix it, picking up any coal that fell out of the bag on the way. After we returned from the coal house I would clean the pram down with water from the hand pump, so that it was ready for the babies to use again.

If they ran out of coal, we would have to join another queue for slack or coke, which was a little cheaper. (Slack was very small pieces of coal and coal dust which would be added to the coal to bank it up and make it last longer. Nothing was wasted, and bags of slack were cheap compared with coal.) I always preferred coal because it created much nicer fires – the coke smelt odd to me but we knew we were lucky just to be warm. In the particularly harsh winters we'd often miss the Saturday matinee we'd been looking forward to because we'd queued so long. By the time we arrived home we were covered in coal dust. We used to wonder whether it was ever worth having a bath the night before on a Friday because we must have looked a right state wandering about the rest of the week covered in coal marks – there are some things a 'lick and a promise' can't conceal! Friday night was bath night though and I don't think we ever bothered trying to negotiate on this.

We had to ration our coal as much as possible. Summers were a blessing because we would only have about one fire roaring in the house on cooler evenings, or for bath night and the furnace in the brick house that heated the copper boiler. But the harsh winters could be horrendous. When we were particularly stretched for fuel there were days when there was no fire in the house at all – those were the worst to endure. It's a type of freezing that thankfully I rarely feel any more but we did somehow adjust, even to those temperatures. We wore our coats indoors and at night would lay them over the top of us. Balaclavas, socks, cardigans and jumpers were necessary additions to night-time winter attire, pulled over nightwear. I wore a liberty bodice on top of my vest to keep me warm too – uncomfortable, but a necessity.

People find it hard to believe that there were three-foot icicles on the insides of our attic window. I admit it makes me laugh a little now as it sounds like something out of a Dickensian tale. But what they find particularly hard to believe is that we used to suck these icicles sometimes too. They looked really rather edible and sherbet-shaped, as if on show in the sweetshop down the road. Keeping the flames alive in our home was central to life as we knew it, but it was Mom who was responsible for getting them started. She was down at six o'clock each morning, before she put the kettle on for the first cuppa of the day. She used her trusty iron companion set – a fork, poker and brush – to sweep the ashes from the grate and start the first fire of the day. The draw tin was used to create a vacuum and make the coal set alight, a task we did from the age of five or six – quickly learning how to hold it properly with an old piece of rag to avoid burning or scarring ourselves. It always amuses me how quick we are to replace everyday household items these days too: our tin kettle, used for everything from boiling up water to making a cuppa, was so worn down that holes eventually began to appear in it.

Because Dad was the ultimate breadwinner our fires tended to revolve around his activity. There were no carpets or flooring in the house either to keep the warmth in. When he was out at the pub or work we huddled around it, taking turns to bask in its warmth. But when he was home it was understood he'd have the main share in his armchair. Sometimes we would forgo a fire during the day until he got home but he was understanding if Mom didn't have enough coal to make one – he understood it was a constant battle to juggle food and fuel.

Dad would try to help Mom out domestically too. The black leaded grate in our fireplace was probably at least a hundred years old and made her life a lot harder because it was difficult to clean. Dad came home one night with some good news: he knew a man who could get us a new mantelpiece and tiled grate that would help to lighten Mom's cleaning load. And we'd be keeping up with those posh people down Coventry Road too!

Not only were they easier to use because the materials were more modern rather than the old cast iron, the tiles would frame an otherwise ordinary fireplace. Dad always had a good eye for aesthetics and design, so this was important to him too. Within a few weeks we were all mucking in to pull out the old one with Dad's tools and our bare hands. Not surprisingly, this was no easy task that took at least half a day. We used all our brute force as we pulled together, choking as we uncovered what was probably about a hundred years' worth of smoke, dust and soot in the process. Afterwards we had to give the whole living room a clear-up – the soot had got into everything, including the wooden table and chenille cloth. But it was worth it though to see the look on Mom's face when the new one was put in. She was so proud that she fetched all the neighbours to have a look. They gathered around it and bent down, cooing at the sight of the beige tiles and shiny new iron grate as though a newborn. To celebrate, we got the toasting fork out and made an inaugural cup of tea and toast to welcome its arrival. Never one to pass up an opportunity to make money, Dad sold the old grate on to the scrapyard. However, our new plush grate should have known it couldn't rest too easy in its new home – turns out it wasn't to be spared the drama of our household. New tiles or not, this meant little to our other inhabitants.

About a month later, when Mom was lovingly cleaning her new grate, a rat happened to run across the hearth. Mom screamed the house down and picked up what was closest to hand, which happened to be the chopper in the coal bucket. She went berserk, swatting at the uninvited rodent aimlessly, not before cracking several of her precious tiles in the process. 'Oh God, what have I done?' she cried. Dad was none too happy when he came home to see the state of our new grate and told Mom she'd have to wait a long time before he retiled it again. Of course the rat escaped scot-free!

7

Coronation Day, Our Brand-New Telly and Grabbing a Tanner for the Meter

As with many items in our household, the wireless was probably a hand-me-down. I've no idea where it came from, but it was definitely a thirties number that might have belonged to Mom's parents or Auntie Lil. This trusty item was situated next to the fireplace and wasn't turned on too often – those weren't the days when the TV and radio were just left on in the background, electricity was far too precious a commodity for that. You were conscious that every bit of the tanner (6d/2.5p) you'd stuck in the meter had to last. But when it did come on, it was regular as clockwork and there was only one person entrusted with turning it on – Dad. At six without fail you'd hear the clunk of the button go on for the news – even more important though was his favourite show, *The Archers*. Dad absolutely lived for that show and never missed an episode. Whenever it was on we had to be as quiet as thieves and if we ever interrupted his daily trip down to Ambridge, there'd been an extra hard clip round the ear 'ole. I'm not quite sure what he loved so much about this programme. He had travelled to some fairly exotic places in his time in the Navy, such as China and Hong Kong, but something about this twenty-minute brief window of time down on the Dorset-based farm left him transfixed. Perhaps it was the simplicity of the countryside in contrast to our urban dwelling. Although they were all sitting round a studio clinking cups, making farmyard noises he truly believed, as does everyone else who listens to the show today, that they were living out a real-life *Countryfile* – another show we're all crazy about today! Dad would sit back in his favourite armchair, light up a Woodbine and give it his full attention, all the while keeping one eye in our direction, just willing us to so much as utter one word. Mom would hover warily by beforehand to remind us in hushed whispers, as if we needed telling, 'Shush, it's *The Archers*!'

I've never been a fan myself. When I married Ray at twenty-one, I soon discovered he also loved it. And it was the same for our kids – they had to be quiet while it was on, on a Sunday, so I've suffered this for 71 years! Well, for better or worse, eh? He even has it on every Sunday morning when he listens to the recording from the week. I can't moan though because he does the ironing while he listens and I stay in bed for a lie-in until it's finished.

I don't know what my dad would have made of the storylines now either. Once upon a time the most exciting cliffhanger was the milk going off, now it's not afraid to shy from all sorts of issues that were once controversial – from domestic violence to gay marriage. Dad listened to it right up until his death in 1983 but I think he would have blown a gasket if he could hear some of the 'racy' goings on now. I can only imagine his bushy eyebrows rising further and further up into his head – 'Political correctness gone mad' is a phrase we might have heard a few times.

As my brother David loved to twiddle with any mechanical items and take them apart, the clock on the mantelpiece was one of his favourites. He knew better than to mess with the reception on the wireless, though. However, he'd invariably receive a clip round the ear 'ole if Dad turned it on and the familial high-spirited tones of the Ambridge theme tune didn't come prancing through quite as crystal clear as he would have liked, bang on the dot of six. It was old and a bit crackly of course, but Dad would normally have adjusted it just as he liked.

So, although we had to remain extremely quiet throughout the news and the blessed *Archers*, it's rare that we took much of it in anyway. We heard words such as 'Suez' and 'Canal', 'Korean' and 'War', 'McCarthy' and 'Witch-hunt' filter through occasionally, spoken in a prim and proper voice that sounded as much a world away from our Brummie tones as the events themselves. They were of little importance to us at the time and the majority of it went over our heads. And it's not as though we were invited for our opinion on these adult affairs either – the culture in our house and indeed the rest of society was still very Victorian. To a large degree the mantra 'Children should be seen and not heard' still resonated. I don't ever remember Dad discussing the headlines with Mom either – more often than not she would be busy with chores or would have rushed off to work in the sausage factory. This is one core reason why I've always encouraged my kids to debate these topics although admittedly, I still command complete silence for *Emmerdale*.

I don't remember the day they announced the death of King George VI particularly. It would have been 1952 of course, the same year seat belts were introduced and the vaccine for polio was created. Everyone seemed to be sad about his death for a while but the lives of the royal families were obviously far removed from us and life continued as normal. I may have heard his voice ringing out on the radio every Christmas or seen his sombre stern face at the end of a British Pathé newsreel, but as a human being he'd made little impact on our lives so far – it's not as though he'd ever visited us in the back-to-backs, had he? However, one event – a direct repercussion of his death – did, despite all the royal protocol and pomp, have a huge impact on me. It contributed to one of the happiest and most cherished days of my life, and for most children of the 1950s: the Queen's Coronation street parties. There are few days that I remember Arthur Street sparkling but on this day in June

1953, it did – the weary grey that always seemed to cloak the street was lifted. The fog and smog so synonymous with post-war rationing and hardship vanished in the sunlight of that afternoon.

It's as though the day itself, bright, sunny and optimistic, nailed a post to the past. Suddenly anything seemed possible and a spirit of optimism swept through our streets. Red, white and blue bunting tied around the lamp posts flurried in the gentle breeze and stretched as far as the eye could see, as though the whole sky was awash with colour and the entire world was celebrating our joy, not just the streets of Small Heath. I think there were times when we felt the outside world had forgotten us on some subconscious level, but there was an inclusive feel to this day – we scrubbed up just as well as those posh houses on Coventry Road. And if you compared our streets they wouldn't have looked too different. I think this was in part because the council provided everyone with the same bunting – I remember men arriving to string it all up. Whatever street you lived on, no one went without: we all shared in this.

Winston Churchill's Conservative government was also happy to encourage this wave of optimism as much as possible. There was still rationing for staple foodstuffs such as sugar, eggs and sausages during the year of Her Majesty's Coronation but the Prime Minister was determined the public would enjoy the day and we were all granted an extra one pound in sugar to help us celebrate, while caterers were also allowed additional sugar and fat. That year, the government also announced the end of sweet rationing – great news for all kids across the country of course because in theory they could buy unlimited amounts of gobstoppers or kali, although we still had to be able to afford them.

I still had no real sense of who this lady was or what she looked like, this woman who at twenty-five was still so young to rule our country. This was obviously before the days when you could just google anyone and although I may have seen her appear at the end of a British Pathé newsreel at the pictures or caught sight of her in my dad's *Birmingham Mail*, we just weren't as saturated with images then. This of course added to her mystery and prestige – I couldn't really identify with this lady but for me she symbolised hope, optimism and a bright new future.

At school, each of us were given a coin, which did help us to feel more connected to her – that this beautiful lady with her noble profile knew we all existed and wanted us to share in the splendour of her day. OK, so there were also many of us who thought 'Ooh, that'll be worth some money one day!' But alas, no such luck. I recently had them valued in the market – they didn't come to much.

For once though, as well as a good chance to have a party, we felt pride on our street. As scruffy, slummy and dead-end as we all were, we felt this was our chance to be noticed and to feel a pride that I don't think we'd felt since the end of the war.

Preparations for the party started much earlier in the year – there wasn't much for us to look forward to in the street

– but I remember clearly that the build-up to the event was just as happy and exciting as the day itself. Although this was an event all communities were going to share in, there was a healthy competitive spirit to the proceedings too. We were all working towards a common goal – Arthur Street was going to put on one of the best parties ever in Small Heath. We were not going to be shown up in front of everyone, not least the Queen, and should she feel inclined to pop by, we'd make sure the cuisine was just as refined as any she would receive at Buckingham Palace and the welcome and atmosphere just as warm – we'd show 'em!

Dad was always one for taking charge but he took to his role as chair of committee for the street party with great enthusiasm. I don't think there was even a vote in the Prince Arthur regarding this one – it was a given that he was the man for the job! And of course, any committee decisions were best made in the pub so happily, he got to spend a bit more time in there than usual. Women were an integral part of the party's success, with plans drawn up and tasks delegated with military precision – often in the brew yard, in between stints in the brick house and hanging out the washing.

Every Saturday, Dad would do the rounds of the neighbourhood to collect money for the party. As it was the end of the week, people would have just been paid. Aside from the Salvation Army, who our community were always happy to give money to, it was a time when everyone seemed happy to part with whatever spare cash they could for the party kitty – there was a real generosity of spirit. I think it's because everyone felt they had a role to play. It was also a chance to witness the creative and artistic talent on the street when they had the money and resources.

Even though flour was still quite a rare commodity, Old Gal Evans and Old Gal Griffin had the opportunity to show off their incredible baking skills – skills that would stand up next to those in *The Great British Bake Off* today, no doubt. I've no idea where these delights were prepared or where they sprung from. You would have thought they'd need a kitchen the size of a palace to produce it all but somehow, from the back of their tiny sculleries, fairy cakes appeared on the day as if by magic, decorated with red, white and blue Union Jacks – the icing and colouring had to be done at the last minute as there were no fridges.

Mom was in charge of the jellies – a particularly rare treat for that day made with hot water heated up on the range. Once set, they had to be eaten fast, which was fine by us kids – we guzzled them down! I don't think I've ever seen so many sandwiches in my life. Rationing had only just finished, so the fillings were still pretty simple – ham, cheese and fish paste – but the sheer quantity was overwhelming. We shared out these little luxuries at the end of the party and there were enough to last a week. It was lovely to savour these treats so long after the celebrations – jellies, cakes and even a pork pie! It's one of those rare times when I remember our appetites being truly sated at the end of the day.

As well as the council helping out with bunting, the church also provided trestles. Several families also risked bringing out their only kitchen table to ensure there were enough seats for what seemed like hundreds of people. The tables were all adorned in blue, white and red ribbons bought from the market or salvaged from wherever possible – all the women and children worked together to help tie the bows. I do remember that Mom was wise enough to put her name at the bottom of our table just in case it went astray. Everyone brought out their plates and dishes to share too, although I remember there were a few terse words towards the end of the day over who owned what! Even the clean-up operation seemed to happen swiftly, as though fairies had swooped down to magically sweep everything away. Because that's how it all felt – magical! Even ordinary everyday items became fantastical – you knew the bog standard chair belonged to Old Gal Evans really, but with a little ribbon and some simple net curtain fabric it was transformed into a velvet and silken throne within the blink of an eye. We had a knack for using our imaginations in those days, with any available resources.

We all sang 'God Save the Queen' in our yard and then the fancy dress contest began – everyone won a prize though because we'd all made such a great effort. We all joined hands and made a circle – one of the girls was the Queen and stood in the middle. We danced around her, singing 'God Save the Queen', and then she sat upon the throne. One of the older boys appointed her the Royal

Highness with one of the crowns we'd made with Auntie Lil. We'd made about fifty or so from sticking beads and bright buttons from her OXO box onto paper to look like jewels. It was incredible how much they twinkled and sparkled, and I still marvel at Auntie Lil's inventiveness – her ability to create anything from a few bits and bobs was astounding.

When we sat down at the long tables in the street to eat all the girls took turns to be crowned. I've never seen so many eager faces keen to get their hands upon a paper hat but we felt that we could be whatever we wanted that day – even the Queen! Finally, we all lined up in the street so that we could toast our new Queen.

Of course, not everyone wanted to dress as the Queen and that was the wonder of it – you could enter into the make-believe of being anybody else, the choice was yours. There were many Roy Rogers running around that day. With his Stetson-wearing, gun-toting swagger, he embodied the genuine cowboy look for many boys of my generation. In 1954 he brought it to the Birmingham Hippodrome, along with his wonderful singing voice and his horse, Trigger. The crowds went wild. My brothers were just as obsessive and dressed up as him for the day, with customised outfits from Auntie Lil. She was incredibly generous with the time she committed to this – as well as making cowboy suits and Indian costumes for the younger boys she made soldier outfits for the others. She helped out with some of the other kids' outfits too.

At the time, I was fascinated by Hawaii and desperately wanted to dress as a Hawaiian girl. I'm not quite sure where this adoration came from. I know my dad had visited there during the war and had talked about the gentle sea breeze of the island with a far-away look in his eye. But I think I must have also seen these exotically beautiful girls, dancing on the beaches, their leis hanging gracefully around them, on Pathé News at the pictures. As well as the snippets of stories I heard from Dad and his foreign adventures, these newsreel documentaries gave a wonderful insight and education into distant lands and the way others lived. I think the films featuring Hawaii stuck with me – whether it was the US President Harry Truman and his family arriving on holiday there, surfers off Mye Lee Beach or young girls showing off their hula skills. Far-off exotic places, a million miles from Arthur Street, where no one was subjected to freezing-cold temperatures or icicles hanging from their windows.

Happily, no one objected to my request or raised an eyebrow at the thought of my skinny little body – we really were all skin and bones then – bracing typical British temperatures in this costume. When I think back now I must have been cold, even though it was June. But I didn't care – I was the only Hawaiian girl on the street that day and I felt incredibly special. Auntie Lil as ever came to the rescue with some woven material she found in the market that she trimmed down and made into a raffia number, as well as a garland of flowers in mixed colours.

I was blessed with long, thick, dark curly hair. It was the envy of my friends at school because I never had to do anything to get it like that. They would badger their moms to replicate the style, toiling with rags and rollers each night. On the flip side, Mom would also occasionally decide to do battle with my hair, attempting to tame it with nothing but a steel comb – it felt like absolute torture! But on this day, it swished from side to side all the way down my back as though I was a genuine hula girl. The finishing touches were the flowers that Auntie Lil weaved through the strands.

The Salvation Army also arrived to provide live music later in the day and I remember us all singing our hearts out to 'God Save The Queen'. Although some of us forgot it wasn't the King any more – oops! Many of the games we played that day are a bit of a blur but I remember Oranges and Lemons, one of our favourite games – the rhyme is permanently stuck in my head too, never to be forgotten:

Oranges and lemons,
Say the bells of St Clement's.
You owe me five farthings;
Say the bells of St Martin's.
When will you pay me?
Say the bells of Old Bailey.
When I grow rich,
Say the bells of Shoreditch.
When will that be?

This is how the game worked: two children would form an arch with their arms, then work out in secret which of them would be an 'orange' and which a 'lemon'. Everyone would then sing the 'Oranges and Lemons' song.

The other children in the game would take turns in running under the arch until one of them was caught when the arch falls at the end of the song. The captured player is asked in secret whether they will be an 'orange' or a 'lemon' and then stands behind the original 'orange' or 'lemon' team leader. The game and singing would then start over again. At the end of the game, there was usually a tug of war to test who was stronger out of the 'oranges' and 'lemons'.

The absolute highlight of this day was watching the Coronation on our brand-new telly, in our very own living room. I've often wondered where the money came from for this luxury, which many, not even the relatively well off could afford, but I suspect it was probably rented off the Coventry Road, which would have cost around £26 a year – I think Dad would have had to put a deposit down. This did make sense at the time because if they broke down the rental business was responsible for repairing them, rather than the owner footing the bill. Of course, it wasn't a question we would have asked back then anyway. Dad was determined that he was going to watch this historic moment on TV and I imagine it was this event that prompted hundreds of Brits to do the same as well. But we were the only ones in up our yard to have this privilege and we could not believe it when Dad came home with a big box the night before. When he opened it and plugged it in to set it up we were all truly amazed – we'd seen them in shop windows down 'The Cov' but never thought we would have one ourselves.

Anyone under the age of fifty would laugh if they saw it today – a model from the USA, I think. The screen measured barely six inches across, with two buttons either side When you turned it on, it made a clunky noise and the picture took at least half a minute to appear. But to us, it was a portal into another world, right here in our own home. This little box perched on our table heralded great technological promise. One of our most prized possessions, it stuck out like a sore thumb amongst so many of the Victorian relics in our home, such as the steel iron and tin kettle. We couldn't believe it and just stood there staring at it, saying over and over: 'What? We've got talking pictures!' We couldn't stop smiling like Cheshire cats, we were so proud.

Word soon spread that we had one and God knows what our neighbours must have thought– either that Dad had robbed a bank or won the Pools. Come three o'clock in the afternoon on Coronation Day, we had the entire street crowding into our front room – from the Bottrells to the Ellises, all staring in disbelief. No one bothered asking and there were no official invitations, but we were all too excited to care – it was every man for himself jostling to take a look at our talking pictures. When I think about it now, there were probably only about thirty people there but it felt as though half the world was sharing in this historic occasion with us.

Mom was dumbfounded but happy too – and for once probably not too concerned with whether her floor looked clean enough. There was no point after everyone had trampled across it anyway! At least now we had something worth nicking, though. I managed to squeeze into a spot on the floor, where I could just about see the whole six inches of screen. Dad delicately adjusted the aerial as though he was some sort of technical professional to make sure the picture and audio were as clear as possible, just as pictures began to beam in from Westminster Abbey. Everyone fell silent. Our little assembled crowd did its best to remain silent throughout the crowning but even Dad didn't dare tick anyone off as we all saw her diamonds, sparkling to such a blinding degree they rivalled the sheen of even my mom's front step – everyone took a sharp intake of breath at the sight of them. 'Can you imagine, all that on your head? Real diamonds!' The hushed whispers spread around the room.

I spared no thought for the Queen's nerves at that moment in time – I was too shaky with pride, both for my country and the spellbound audience we had attracted to our little realm at 3/84. It was so rare for us to own an item no one else had, Dad was definitely pleased to be the envy of the street for once, too.

In hindsight, who knows how she must have felt to

have so many eyes on her – not least half of Small Heath. I often wonder now what was going through her mind. She managed to look so calm, serene and noble as they balanced what must have felt like half a tonne of bricks upon her head.

It felt as though we watched the Queen for hours but in truth I think it was only about five minutes – distracting as the sight of Her Majesty was, we soon got back to the more urgent and pressing work of carrying the food and drink out for the street party before any of it melted. Typically, as everyone trooped out, Mom cast an eye over the clear-up she'd have to do in her living room. In hindsight, the TV may have seemed something of an extravagance to her, especially as our family lived in poverty, but once Dad had got used to it, that was it, there was no going back. And we spent many a happy hour in front of that box so it was worth it. It wasn't quite like a family sitting round the box now – there were no sofas to lounge on and us kids would be settled on the flagstone floor, which was incredibly cold, hard and bare to sit on, even with one of Dad's rugs put down. And although we had to be quiet during the news, which was always switched on at six, we used to be in fits of laughter on the rare occasion we all watched *I Love Lucy* as a family. If Mom was at work, Dad would often watch with us while he was busy woodcarving – before he went to the pub he found time to make footstools, tables, cupboards or cribs, or we'd help him thread his rugs.

After school, TV was probably our favourite, though.

One series that I particularly remember was *Watch With Mother*, a cycle of children's programmes, broadcast of course by the only network at that time, the BBC. It first started broadcasting in 1953, the same year as the Coronation, and was a follow-on from their radio version, *Listen With Mother*. Interestingly, it was intended 'to deflect fears that television might become a nursemaid to children and encourage bad mothering'. *Andy Pandy*, *The Flower Pot Men*, *Picture Book* and *The Woodentops* were all firm favourites of ours and we used to love singing along to the *Muffin the Mule* songs.

Generally, Mom was too busy to ever actually watch these programmes with us – the titles held more relevance for stay-at-home, middle-class moms with time on their hands – though she would inevitably end up learning some of the songs and getting them stuck in her head as she hurried to get dinner ready. She may perhaps have agreed to some extent about the bad parenting fears as well (along with the old 'square eyes' myth), because we weren't allowed to watch too much TV. Instead, she preferred us to play outside in fresh air, which she used to say would do us the world of good, though I suspect she didn't want the whole lot of us under her feet for too long either.

And of course there was the ongoing problem of making sure there was enough electricity in the meter. We had two separate rusting 'shilling in the slot' meters – one for gas and one for electricity. We'd place coins in on the left side, then turn a dial to see how much gas or electricity was left. The gas man would come to empty the meter and occasionally gave us a refund if we'd paid over on the amount of gas we'd actually used – Mom would gladly take the cash. However, the TV tended to guzzle our electricity so the chances of it running out halfway through one of Dad's favourite programmes or God forbid, *The Archers*, was a distinct possibility. And sometimes it ran out in the middle of Mom cooking the tea. This always provoked arguments about whose turn it was to go and beg the neighbours for help, a task we all dreaded, because it often meant disturbing them while they were eating. We would bang on the nearest door and ask if they could lend us a shilling till pay day, or if they had any change for two tanners (sixpences). Mr Bottrell was always kind and obliging, especially when he saw the desperate looks on our faces or if we were standing out in the cold. It was embarrassing, but needs must. There was certainly never a dull moment in our household – we were always kept on our toes! However, if it was in the middle of one of Dad's programmes we were under extra pressure – we didn't want him to get angry about missing the entire show. The worst was when we had to go out in extreme weathers: we'd run out in the snow or rain to find a kindly neighbour who would take pity. By the time we got back, we would often be soaked through. Dad would look up and say, 'Where the bloody hell you been, China and back?' If only…

We didn't dare answer back though or we'd get a clip

round the ear 'ole! Sometimes it made little difference as the boys often received one anyway if they'd missed some important bit of news. I do sometimes think it's amazing my older brothers have their ears left. We found out years later once we'd left the back-to-backs that David actually had a burst eardrum. Mom would rightly go mad if Dad forgot and automatically reached for his ear 'ole, as was the age-old habit. There were certainly more cons than pros to having an electricity meter and I count my blessings that the days of scurrying around for a spare tanner are well and truly behind me.

8

Green Lane Bath House and Library

On the corner of Green Lane and Little Green Lane, just off the Coventry Road, stands the original site of the Small Heath Public Library and Baths. A fairly short fifteen-minute walk for us from Arthur Street, it's a beautiful Grade II-listed building that opened as a library, with bathing facilities added later in 1902. Designed by architects William Martin and John Henry Chamberlain, the building mixed red brick with terracotta. Although converted into a mosque back in 1979, it still has its original Victorian features – the Gothic decorative wrought-iron patterns around a tall circular clock tower always reminded me of a turret out of a fairytale. Growing up, it was a very special place to me for that reason – as well as being a beautiful spacious building it housed books that transported me to another magical fairyland. But it was also special because it's one of the places where I indulged in my own luxurious bath, not too dissimilar from later experiences swanning about in a hot tub. The baths were a definite treat, though – we'd only go about once a month if Mom could spare a few pennies and we'd completed our chores.

Dennis and David's first trip was instigated by Dad, who decided as they were in their early teens they should both use them. I think this was his way of suggesting they were entitled to a bit more modesty at this age than they were ordinarily used to during bath night down Arthur Street. And it was also a way of giving Dennis more responsibility. It was huge kudos for both him and David to be given extra money on a Friday night and you could see they felt like all the other grown-up lads who went there with their parents, so it was a sign of their burgeoning maturity. I was keen to tag along with the boys, not wanting to miss out on this experience. I was also starting to go through puberty at the age of eleven so Mom decided it was the right time for me to go as well, which put an end to the tin baths at home too – I can't say I missed them much! But my first experience of the baths was a rather bewildering one for me, particularly after all those years of bathing by the fire.

I don't think the boys were too keen to have me tagging along with them in all honesty and were happy to wave goodbye to me as I joined the separate entrance for women.

It felt a bit strange to be segregated – I was so used to the inclusive atmosphere at home and not having any privacy in front of the lads. It was also rather scary to wander in on my own. But these feelings were soon overtaken as I was hit by a blast of steam and wonderful smells that instantly struck me as I walked through. The bath halls, with their cast-iron columns and shafts and tinted glass windows, reminded me of something from Roman times or a glamorous spa location off Pathé News.

It all seemed so enormous to me at the time. When the female attendant handed me a towel she looked a little amused by my expression. To me the concept of having my own towel was pretty alien. When she also gave me my own bar of carbolic soap, I looked around as if to say, 'What, just for me? All of it for me?' It seemed like a waste. I kept expecting Mom to grab it out of my hands and tell me 'Time's up!' or for Barbara to begin crying when she got too cold, waiting for her turn in the bath. Here, the bath was deep and clinical so I felt a little lost in it. I wasn't used to having more than six inches to play with so it took a while for me to relax and I didn't stay in it for long, so new was this experience.

I kept expecting the lady to come in and tell me to hurry up and get out because someone else needed to get in. It also never occurred to me to run the water out either – I was so used to other people sharing it. When I got out and put my own dry towel around me, another new novelty in itself, she came in to clean the bath. She was none too pleased to see this and looked at me pointedly before snapping: 'Oh dear, you left all the dirty water in.' She tutted when she pulled the plug out and washed it out with some sort of flashy chemical liquid I'd not seen before. Not before turning to me to remark: 'And what did your last slave die off?'

To me, it seemed so strange to watch her pull the plug out and waste all of that water – Mom would have bathed six kids in there and then got in herself. But the next week I felt a lot more confident. I knew the system a little better and didn't feel quite so nervous as I took my own towel and bar of soap. Now I tried to relax and imagine that I was a film star lounging in there or I'd just been blessed with some magical treat. Each time I grew more and more confident and was soon staying in for at least twenty minutes at a time. I really enjoyed the fact I could take my time and not have to worry about sharing one bit of flannel. I even washed my hair in there with the remaining piece of soap. I thought I'd died and gone to heaven, I could have stayed in there all day! The boys were always out before me.

There were two swimming pools at the baths. They were probably each only about fifteen by ten feet but they seemed huge the first time I went and everything echoed around me in there – the sounds of people shouting and laughing. As I didn't know how to swim, I hung back and watched Dennis and David enjoying themselves. I was really impressed they could both swim but was terrified by the prospect of getting in – it looked so cold and uninviting. I dipped my toe tentatively in the water as Dennis laughed and said, 'Oh, don't be such a baby, get in, you'll love it!' He'd promised to teach me to swim a few weeks before but it turned out his methods were from the standard big brother school of teaching – I screamed as he pushed me in and I felt the water shoot up my nose. It was a horrible experience as I splashed and splayed around in there. I jumped out and gave him a good talking to.

The next time I went, I took Ann and Valerie. The lads were much nicer to us this time and left us to it in the shallow end. Then they showed us how to float and splash our legs using a white floater. They were always trying to get us to swim down to the deeper end but it took time to learn – I was never that good, but I was proud that I could finally swim and had overcome my fear. They were some of the happiest times that I remember, messing around in that pool – shouting, laughing and having fun, it felt good to be alive. I think it's fantastic these places existed for the public and gave kids like us the opportunity to experience beautiful Victorian buildings that were a part of the city's heritage.

I absolutely loved going to the library next door, not only because it housed so many books, it was peaceful – people only spoke in whispers, which my brothers struggled with, so they were often told off by the librarian. But even I, as something of a known chatterbox, managed to keep quiet. And I loved the solitude. To me it seemed so big, with its towering rows of bookcases and quiet, long oak tables for people to sit at and pore over books and reference maps for hours. It was typically Victorian, with its solid thick walls and high rectangular windows that let in plenty of light. At one end was a giant map of the world on a banner strung up with pulleys that took up half the room. There was a sculpture of a group of figures in medieval and Renaissance dress that symbolised 'Learning, Knowledge and Study' too. I also loved the smell of polish – different to Mom's carbolic red potion but just as strong.

It was a treat to have all this space away from our little house. I loved to wander up and down, taking ages to choose my books. The boys would always get theirs as quickly as possible but I loved to take my time, so I preferred going with friends. There weren't many books in our home – for a start, there really wasn't the space for them and Mom didn't have the time to read. But I loved taking out the maximum amount – up to three at a time – and was keen to learn. My favourites were Enid Blyton's *Famous Five* and the *Secret Seven* series. I adored any stories with fairies in them too – anything that transported me into another world.

In my early teens I had a friend whose relative worked at Cadbury's – I think they may have lived at the Bournville site, the model village on the south side of Birmingham, built by John Cadbury himself. She had the most incredible huge box of chocolates that we loved – not just for the chocolates (which we made ourselves violently sick on) but the vivid picture of a country cottage on the front, with flowers and fairies dotted around it. Even now I have fairy ornaments in the garden of my present home and at the bottom of my rockery around the big oak tree – there is a hole in the bottom for them to fly in and out of at their leisure. Each one is named after my three grandchildren and five great-grandchildren. I love them because they transport me back to the corner of that library where my sister Barbara and I loved reading for hours. Tucked away in a safe little haven, it was an escape for us and we thought it was wonderful to have all this choice for free. I think it's a shame so many libraries are closing as they did give many children this opportunity. They were the most magical books to get lost in and even now, I get completely lost in a book once I've picked it up.

1

Friday Night is
Bath Night

Bath time is one of life's most undisputed pleasures and as much as it's become an everyday pastime in our modern lives, it's certainly a joy I never take for granted. Whenever I ease my way into a relaxing bubble bath that's brimming with a blend of my favourite Radox scents to soothe away any troubles of the day – magnolia and patchouli, to be precise – the memories of bath-time living in the back-to-backs are a stark contrast to what I enjoy now.

Then there's Michelle, my daughter, who keeps a hot tub in her garden – beautifully warm all year round. It's an absolute joy to laze and swim in and enjoy a tipple or two in. My favourite on a ladies-only night is vodka with fresh orange and plenty of ice – wonderful to savour while having a joke and a giggle with all our girly friends. As we all enjoy a drink at the end of the week they'd find it hard to believe how different Friday night was for me all those years ago.

Yes, Friday night was always bath night. When I visited the restored back-to-backs, our guide said it was fortnightly for some families – certainly not ours, it was a regular weekly occurrence for the Rainbirds and it was tough work for both Mom and Dad. It may be a long time ago now but I can still feel the mottled base of the tin bath on my feet as I edged tentatively into the water – it was never of course adjusted to the perfect tried-and-tested temperature I enjoy today. And the tin would get scorching hot by the fire – you soon learnt if you let your arm dangle over the side of the bath!

Not only was it physically hard work but time was most certainly of the essence with up to seven children for Mom to wash at one point – there was a lot of water to get warm. First of all, she would normally have two pots of heated water on the go – one on the stove in the scullery and another heating up in the galvanised pot on the black leaded fire grate. This was to fill the bath as quickly as possible before it went cold. The whole system was overseen by Mom with such regimented precision it wasn't too dissimilar to an army barracks at ours on a Friday night. I think Dad's naval training must have helped with this, too – we all had our orders and things got going extremely quickly. But to lift and fill the pots was an exhausting and tiring job. Mom did this, even when she was expecting, which seemed to be at least once a year throughout the early fifties. As the eldest kids, Dennis, David, Alan and I would help out between us in turn, in pairs.

Of course, there was the age-old important question of who should be bathed first to benefit from the cleanest water. For some families it depended on who was the dirtiest but us Rainbirds always went in according to birth order. Dennis and David would get in first – one of the rare perks for Dennis as head of the household, who was chuffed to bits to have this luxury. I'd be juggling for space with my younger brother Alan, although the fight for room was normal in any part of life in our home and indeed, within our entire upbringing. I always remember that the water barely came up to my belly button so there wasn't much to play with, not that we had the time to have a good splash around. Occasionally, Mom would top up the water throughout our bathe but normally only for the little ones. A bit of extra water didn't make the experience any more pleasurable but obviously we didn't know any different – bath time was not a time of relaxation!

Dennis and David would be scruffy and ingrained with dirt from their week's escapades or sometimes even from the chimney sweeping that they used to help Dad with. Although our water wasn't fresh, Alan and I counted ourselves lucky to get in when we did! Because after that came Barbara and the little ones. By the time they hopped out, the water would be black. Sometimes, when the babies were really small, it was easier and more hygienic to wash them in the sink in the scullery.

Carbolic soap was always on standby and an absolute staple for cleanliness – not only in the wash house but in the bath too. Also to the rescue came a piece of old towel – nothing was thrown away in those days, everything could be 'upcycled'. I still find it hilarious that on a recent trip to Shoreditch in London they served cocktails out of jam jars – they were a necessity for us because we couldn't afford proper drinking mugs or glasses but now they're trendy!

So, a lowly old fragmented bit of towel was transformed into a flannel – no trips for such added luxuries to Woolworths, I'm afraid. This was quickly rubbed over the face followed by a lightning-speed hair wash – with our thick black curly hair this could sometimes be painful and I don't think it really got the thorough clean it needed. Mom would stand over us, ensuring we got out as quickly as possible. We'd ease ourselves out, careful not to upset the bath or cause any spills. I don't think there was ever much of a negotiation on who got out first – it wasn't as unsteady as exiting a hammock but the experience wasn't that sturdy if one of us made a rush for it either, so you had to be careful! Occasionally, she would top up the water throughout our bath but that didn't make the experience any more pleasurable – obviously we didn't know any different but I felt for the little ones left in at the end in all that black water.

Now, every time I bathe I have the luxury of leaving my

bath exactly where it is: in the sanctuary of my bathroom. No such joy for us back then. The hard work of bath night wasn't over once we'd got through the first stage and it couldn't be left in front of the fire. By the end of the night it was hung up in the coal house but before that it was carried by Mom, Dad, Dennis and me to empty down a drain outside. It was quite a regular occurrence to see other families struggling to carry heavy tins of bath water on a Friday night. Even though there were four of us we'd all be staggering about, carrying it as though it was some sort of coffin across the court. It wasn't the easiest of tasks and it was difficult not to spill on occasions, inside the house as well as outside. Down the empty drain it would go, all the dirt and slosh. Then we'd give it a quick clean in the scullery and one of us would carry it back down to the coal 'ole. After that, Mom would rush off to the sausage factory for her 6pm shift while Dad would change into his suit to go to the pub across the road for 9pm. It was always a quick turnaround on Friday night.

So, a house with a bath was a palace in our eyes, and most certainly, as we would say, posh – even if you weren't that much better off than us. My husband Ray is one such example. His family weren't particularly well off, but bath night is yet another experience that would have made his eyes pop out, not least for some of its more frantic moments too.

One Friday night when I was about seven I was at one end of the bath with Alan at the other. I needed a wee but

I didn't want to get out and trail up the yard to the toilet – it was so cold and dark and meant getting out of the bath that I'd started to warm myself in, in front of the coal fire. So, rather than considering the consequences, I relieved myself in the bath – my indiscretion was not hidden, of course. The water went bright yellow, not unlike what happens when you throw in one of today's bath bombs!

My dad came in and noticed straight away. He slapped Alan with the back of his hand and said: 'You dirty bugger!' He then went to slap him again. The injustice of this caused me to cry out: 'Don't hit him, it was me!'

Mom came in to hear the shouting and said we'd have to boil up some fresh water – what a palava! She sent one of the kids to fetch the doctor, suspecting I was ill. Dr Macintosh's surgery was off 'The Cov', about five minutes away. We were lucky, in emergencies we could call him out – we didn't have a phone so Dennis or David would run down the road to call him. When he arrived, he told her I had yellow jaundice.

I was sent to bed for several days nursing fever, chills, headache and muscle aches. Most of all though I remember being very bored, up there in the attic with no one to play with or talk to. I could hear my siblings outside in the yard, shouting and laughing, which added to my woes.

Any other night, we'd have a quick swill under the tap in the sink in the scullery. We had no hot running water so it was always cold – we'd wash our face, arms, neck and ears. This was a routine we continued in the

Above left: A studio portrait of Maureen's mother, Ruby, with Ray, dear Auntie Lil's son.

Above right: Auntie Lil (Lil Bryan, born 1906), Maureen's mom's half-sister. A very important figure in Maureen's and her mother's lives, she had become a mother figure to Ruby when she lost her own mother at the age of six.

Below left: Fond memories: Valerie and Ann Nee, Maureen's best friends in the back-to-backs. They lived at the bottom of the entry on the front of Arthur Street.

Below right: Left to right: friends Jacqueline, Pat and Maureen, aged eleven, with Santa, Christmas 1957.

Left: An electric trolley bus at the bus depot at the end of Arthur Street, where it joins Coventry Road. Auntie Lil worked here, cleaning the buses.

Right: Maureen's mother with Uncle Ray, Auntie Lil's son.

Left: Oh boy, oh boy! – a young boy receiving his *Daily Mail* boots. Not very attractive items, they were nevertheless strong and serviceable, and had metal studs in the soles – great in snow or ice.

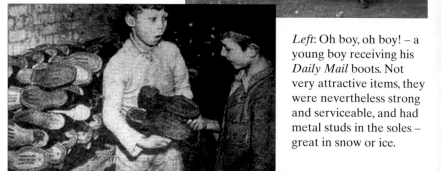

Right: These boots are made for working: sturdy and work-ready, the free *Daily Mail* boots, available only to men and boys, proved a fundamental accessory for the labouring man. They would be something of a fashion statement today, too.

Left: A depiction of the back-to-back housing of the kind in which Maureen was brought up. Cramped, hastily built with inadequate materials, and condemned as unfit for purpose as early as the 1870s, they were nevertheless the homes of the increasingly emergent working-class population in major cities.

(The Back-to-Backs of Birmingham, watercolour by Beryl Evans)

Right: A preserved courtyard of a back-to-back in Birmingham. The washing would be hung out even when still wet, because of the damp in the housing; note the outdoor 'lavs' (toilets) in the background. The last surviving back-to-back courtyard in Birmingham, of the thousands built, is now a museum run by the National Trust.

Left: 'The Salvation Army, who our community were always happy to give money to' – the Army's band processing through the streets on a Sunday, closely followed by Boy Scouts, Girl Guides and Brownies singing and tapping tambourines; they were hard to miss.

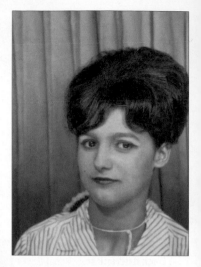

Above left: A British summer holiday – Maureen and her mother at Weston-super-Mare, 'suitably named "Weston-super-Mud".' The family's van only reached the resort thanks to Mom's stockings, deployed as a makeshift fan belt.

Above right: Maureen aged sixteen – in the days before the selfie, the photo booth provided everything from passport photos to self-portraits, for a few shillings, although you had to wait several minutes for the strip of four photos to be developed.

Below left: A much treasured photo-booth shot of Maureen and her husband Ray shortly after they married in 1967; at that date her youngest brother, Kevin, was only four, and she twenty-one.

Below right: Maureen with her grandson Jordan in the brewus of the restored back-to-backs in Birmingham, with the boiler at right and the mangle (wringer) at left. It was Jordan's interest that inspired Maureen to write this book.

morning, which we called a 'lick and a promise' – Mom was very adamant that we all did this before dinner too or when we came in from playing, no matter the weather or however cold it was. We got used to this daily ritual and even now I like to splash my face with a bit of cold water, even in freezing temperatures.

Occasionally throughout the week though, we'd also have what's called a 'strip wash'. This was where we'd boil water on the stove and strip down to our underwear. Sometimes I would wash my hair if I knew the nit nurse was on the prowl at school. Nits were a common problem growing up at school but Mom and I would try to combat them as much as possible with some disgusting yellow smelly stuff to keep the buggers away – I think we used to get it from the welfare. It wasn't always easy to get the nit comb through my curly black hair, so my scalp would be rubbed raw sometimes.

Now of course, bath time is a completely different experience for me, not least because I no longer have to share with Alan! But more than this, I also appreciate what an enjoyable experience bath time is for me and my great grandchildren – it's a time for playing, fun and affection, as well as an opportunity for quality bonding time. I love nothing more than to hear their chuckles and see their grins as they stare transfixed at the sight of a yellow duck squeezing water or me quacking away, doing silly expressions. I enjoy snuggling them afterwards in warm towels and drying in between their toes. Unfortunately,

Mom didn't have the time to indulge in this. Now I'm not knocking her at all, she was very loving and cared deeply for us, but sadly, she couldn't ever really be present with us. It's interesting to recognise and explore these contrasts with today, but to also feel gratitude for the time I have to enjoy and indulge in these precious moments, as many other mothers and grandmothers do.

From as young as I can remember I would help out with many aspects of what I suppose you would call childcare today. With very little space in the house, every surface was a precious commodity so our table, although used primarily for family meals, was also the centrepiece for just about every other activity – therefore was not spared from nappy changing. So, if a Terry nappy wasn't drying on the fireguard it was often to be found here, with me doing my best to wrestle a baby into one.

There were a couple of close misses when they nearly rolled off the table as the babies got bigger – it became a lot harder for me to hold them while changing nappies on the table. When it came to bath night, I was in charge of helping out with towel rotation. Towels certainly weren't as bright or as fluffy as they are today, in part because it was tough to get them dry – one of my pet peeves is towels that have been dried on a line and I think it stems from this. I love it when they are all fresh and bouncy, straight out of the dryer – it's my favourite modern appliance and I'd choose one over a dishwasher any day.

Mom always got what she could from the club man but

we were not blessed with individualised towels for each child, we had about three or four towels to share between the seven of us, which added to the challenges and stresses of bath night. She was often losing the battle to keep the towels dry and ensure that all the children were dried adequately too. Because they were in constant use our towels would often make us even wetter than we already were. As each pair got out of the bath, we'd try to dry ourselves as quickly as possible in front of the fire, dress and then dry the towels in front of the fire ready for the next two. Mom would also try to solve the problem by drying them on the table, as well as attempting to air them with our two steel irons – no doubt because they actually were Victorian. She used this same technique for drying sheets too, which was another constant battle for her.

Mom couldn't stand ironing, and avoided it where possible, other than cleaning the towels and sheets. I take after her in that respect. Thankfully my husband Ray is much happier doing it. Back then though, it was a necessary task that every dutiful wife had to perform, particularly when it came to her husband's shirts. Dad had a couple that we got from the club man, which he'd wear either for work or to look smart on a Saturday for the pub.

However, Dad's shirts would often have scorch marks on them from where the iron had got incredibly hot from heating up on the fire. From the age of five I became quite a dab hand at picking up the iron to help Mom out with the drying system. However, there were no oven gloves in those days, at least certainly not in our house – we would use a mere piece of rag. I learnt quickly to always remember to use it, as there were a number of times I burnt myself badly when I forgot so it was not uncommon to catch a glimpse of one of these marks on Dad's shirts, though in hindsight I wonder if Mom was getting revenge for this thankless chore – and one of her least favourites!

The endless washing and drying was the bane of her life, particularly of course on wash day – getting things dry and aired was a continual struggle in the good old British climate, though I never heard her particularly complain. But her main motivation for drying everything so scrupulously was because she didn't want us to catch colds or get rheumatism. It can't have been easy when she saw us suffering with various fevers and colds that she must have known were exacerbated, or even caused, by poor living conditions in the house. I feel for her, but she did the best she could to protect us.

As I've said, Mom didn't always express how much she cared for us through big hugs or kisses – parents are a lot more demonstrative these days, which I think is a good thing as love is fundamentally important for any child. But I think her tireless attempts to ensure we stayed as warm and dry as possible were her way of showing us.

10

Rescuing Dad's Suit from the Pawn Shop, Visiting the Moneylender and Witnessing Chicken Slaughter

When it came to other financial saviours in our life, who were of more practical help than any well-meaning nuns, it was the pawn shop and the moneylender who came to our rescue. Those visits were another Monday speciality, certainly a busy day for me and Mom. But it was this visit down to the Coventry Road that I probably dreaded the most. The familiar three brass balls hanging outside were a brazen reminder that you were definitely in the right place. Many people on my street went to pawn shops – it was a humiliating but necessary experience for a lot of us, but again it was something that we all preferred to keep 'hush hush'. People seemed to carry quite a strong sense of shame around when it came to their financial matters. Each time I went, I'd pray for dear life I wouldn't meet anyone I knew.

The tell-tale sign was anyone carrying Yardley sheets under their arm – if they were all washed and wrapped up in brown paper, everyone knew where you were going! We pawned many items – Dad's selection of silk pyjamas he brought back from his travels often made an appearance in there. But more often than not, it was his precious weekend suit that I took in at Mom's request. However, Dad was completely in the dark about this. Unbeknownst to him, it spent more time in the pawn shop all week, Monday to Friday, than it ever did on his back.

This was the main reason I struggled with this chore. It was yet another secret, bundled up in brown paper this time, but it was one I had to keep from Dad. I hated being caught in the middle of their financial difficulties and the lies it forced me to tell. On the Monday I would pawn his suit for two and six – 12.5p, but equivalent to £3.25 in today's money. With that you could easily buy a pound of margarine, a loaf of bread and a dozen eggs so Mom would use it to put towards the housekeeping.

Every Friday lunchtime she would send me on the bus to the Morris Minor car factory, where Dad now worked in Drew's Lane, Washwood Heath, roughly two miles north-east of the city centre. In 1959 the Morris Minor became the first British car to sell a million but this site hadn't always been used for this purpose. During World War I the factory produced munitions even though it was originally designed as a car plant to assemble the Wolseley Stellite. In the twenties it was bought out by William Morris and Morris Minor engines were produced there from the thirties onwards.

Everyone we knew worked in shops or factories and Dad was no different. He was a shop steward there throughout most of the fifties and fortunately it was a regular job, at least until the strikes that were to bedevil the British motor industry for decades. As well as providing a steady income, the factory helped to create a sociable and fun atmosphere for its employees at its working man's club. Occasionally on a Sunday, Dad would take me, Dennis and David there. As well as a bar they had a separate concert room that children were allowed into. We enjoyed going there for a change and a treat. Dennis had heard that if you sang on stage you would receive sixpence. As ever, he was up for it as another potential means to raise cash. David and I were not so keen but Dennis was never a shy one! And he managed to persuade us.

We went into a corner and rehearsed 'Que Sera Sera' (Doris Day's hit that came out in 1956) for all of ten minutes before we got up to sing our little hearts out. Dave and I were red-faced and nervous, which no doubt affected our performance – somebody sensitively told me I was 'a little flat and too near the mic'. But Dennis saved the day with his confident swagger and we each received a sixpence – we were thrilled. But when it came to Dad's suit we couldn't afford to take the 'Que Sera Sera' approach –

Mom and I had to stick to a tight schedule for this one.

As I waited for Dad to come out of the gate at the factory with his pay packet, I'd prepare myself for his angry response. It was a Friday so he'd just been paid and when he saw my nervous little face he knew I'd be asking for money. I always felt a little like Oliver Twist as I asked him for housekeeping. He felt humiliated in front of his colleagues and would say: 'Tell your mom I will have words with her, sending you down here, showing me up in front of me mates.' But luckily he never asked me specifically what it was for – I don't think I could have lied directly to his face. If he'd ever found out that we needed the money to buy back his beloved suit then I think he would have hit the roof! It was crucial of course that we did get it back before the week was out – time was of the essence as the shop closed at five and Dad would want to wear it that evening.

Once I had the cash in my hands I would rush to the pawn shop and pay for the clothes to be returned. Now, I chuckle a little at the thought of Dad smartening himself up to go down the pub, none the wiser that his suit had been languishing in the pawn shop only a few hours earlier, but at the time I found juggling this web of deceit stressful and upsetting, especially because he took it out on me, and I was only doing what Mom asked me to, to help her out.

When I was home I would repeat what Dad had said to Mom and vow to myself this was the last time I was going to do it – I felt ashamed and a lowlife. When Dad returned there was the inevitable row. She would say: 'If you want to eat, then you have to provide the money.' And he would reply: 'I can't give you what I ain't got.' Other than win the pools, there wasn't a lot that she could do to alter the situation though, so the games continued for years. If one sibling moaned loud enough about a chore it would inevitably be passed around to another.

I didn't like to complain about my visits to the pawn shop but I think Mom did realise how much it got to me, so David took up the challenge on a Friday. I was relieved to take a break from it, but wondered what it would be replaced with. Not surprisingly, it involved money, but at least it meant a change of routine and scenery. This time it took me to a street just down by the Kingston Picture House on Coventry Road. It opened in 1935 and was one of our most favourite places to visit as kids. Although it had a fairly ordinary brick façade the white-stoned columned centrepiece lent a glamorous feel. We loved nothing better than to nestle in the back stalls of the auditorium, with its grand Art Deco-inspired hanging light in the middle, to watch the latest Roy Rogers film. Those were the cheapest seats of course, at around sixpence. If we could afford it, we'd buy a bag of chips afterwards from Bolton Road for three pence. They were soaked in chip fat, like burnt bits with batter stuck to them, wrapped in newspaper, which always seemed to make them taste better. We'd save any paper to make a fire in the brewus.

But there were to be no visits to the cinema this time. I was off to see the moneylender. She turned out to be a pleasant, plump lady with a genuine smile, so the change of chore was welcome to some degree. She had the kind of house we kids could only have dreamed about – a front room parlour, living room and small kitchen at the back. Definitely posh! I think I felt immediately felt safe because she smelt of Lily of the Valley, which was Auntie Lil's perfume of choice too.

It turned out Mom had been borrowing money for several years. This was yet another secret that I never knew was going on. I visited this lady quite a few times – we used to borrow about two shillings and six pence (12.5p). Although profiting from other people's misfortune, she was always kind to me. She seemed to take pity on me and always gave me an extra penny to spend on sweets as she handed over the cash in a brown envelope and told me to 'take care'. I have no comprehension of the rates she was charging, I would never have understood or asked such a question anyway – for all I know they could have been extortionate, not too dissimilar to payday loans. But neither Mom nor Dad would have visited a bank – and I don't think they ever held an account until decades after we lived in the back-to-backs.

As far as I know, Dad never knew anything about this so it was another secret to keep. It was Mom's means of survival and most of the people we knew did the same when things got tough and they had a big family to support.

The year 1953 is remembered for many happy events – namely, the end of rationing and the Coronation.

But it wasn't such a good year if you were a rabbit or a fan of eating this extremely popular meat. That spring, Myxomatosis broke out across the country, a viral disease that rapidly killed tens of millions of them. My grandchildren are surprised that rabbits were so widely available – they just know them as cute and fluffy pets. It was a popular staple in our house: not only was it packed full of nutrients and vitamins, it was relatively cheap in comparison to chicken and turkey. We'd buy it from the market normally – I can see rabbits hanging up on hooks as if it were yesterday – and Mom would cook up a tasty stew that would last the week.

But our love affair with rabbit ended when the virus took its toll and we needed to look for other meats to take its place. Chicken is incredibly common now but back then it was a lot more expensive and still viewed as a relative luxury. Therefore, anyone who owned chickens was deemed as pretty well off, as was the case with Mrs Griffin, who lived in the back of 80, across the yard from us. Their house was similar to ours but as she just lived with her husband, she had a little more space. She owned about twenty chickens that were kept in a small, fenced-off yard in front of their house. She was a kind lady though and gave us the odd egg occasionally or tuppence in exchange for leftover potato and vegetable peelings. Mrs Griffin had a hearty stature that seemed more suited to labour in the countryside than toiling away in the yard of the back-to-back – I could easily have pictured her down on the farm, nonchalantly lugging about a dead carcass or two. We knew she didn't keep the chickens as pets and the boys and I often wondered when she decided their time was up down Arthur Street, but nothing prepared us for the sight of what we were about to see one day in her yard, when she employed Dad to sweep the chimney. This was quite a regular gig and I think some of our kindlier neighbours would take him and the lads on, even if they didn't necessarily need the help.

Because the back-to-backs were made of brick, they were better able to withstand the high temperatures that were reached from domestic fires. By the eighteenth century most chimneys were built with twelve-inch flues and this size was reduced even more to nine by nine inches, which was only one brick by one brick. The flues in the chimneys of the back-to-backs would not have been that much bigger, hence why Dad often took Dennis or David with him as it was easier for them to reach their arms up and get into the cracks. The tools they used hadn't moved on much from Victorian times either, as they used fairly basic black brushes of various sizes.

I was never tasked with the hard graft of cleaning the flue but I loved to accompany them on their job. My favourite part of this was waiting for the big black brushes to peep out through the chimney. I would keep going outside to check, then I would jump up and down excitedly and run back in, shouting to let them know they were finally through. It seemed as though we waited hours sometimes.

My dad and brother would arrive home, covered in black soot, coughing and spluttering – Mom was never too happy to see us after our trips back. Dad did his best to stop the soot from getting everywhere. He'd put old rags and newspapers down all around the fireplace but we would all be absolutely filthy when we returned, the soot ingrained in our hair, clothes and nails. I always thought it would be easier to have a bath but we had to settle for a strip wash in the scullery with pink carbolic soap because Mom was always conscious of the cost of heating the water.

I don't know how much Dad would receive for this job but he was good at most things he turned his hand to, especially anything practical. When he went to clean Mrs Griffin's chimney, it was nearly Christmas so she offered him a chicken for our Christmas dinner instead of money. This was actually very kind of her as a whole chicken would have been worth quite a bit more than the actual payment and we were delighted at the prospect of eating this delicious meat – what a treat for us! There was one condition, though: Dad had to catch it first. She gestured out to the yard, where at least six chickens were minding their own business in the cold winter air.

With his years in the Navy, Dad didn't look at all fazed at the thought of catching a chicken and strolled out confidently in the direction of the first one that caught his eye. 'Come 'ere!' he said as he strode towards it. Well, the chicken was having none of it and showed little respect for this man who'd fought for Queen and Country. We all fell about laughing in hysterics as the battle ensued – expletives poured forth from Dad's mouth as the chicken cleverly evaded his grabbing hands. It was rare to see Dad flustered by anything but here he was, trouser legs akimbo amidst a sea of feathers. How quickly the tears of laughter turned to those of horror though as Dad's caveman instincts kicked in – or at least his desire for a really good decent piece of chicken breast at Christmas.

It turns out that Dad must have learnt how to kill a chicken at some point in his life as he proved pretty adept at it once he got his hands on it. Like something out of a Ray Mears' TV programme, we froze as he wrung its neck in front of us then took it to the back of the scullery to chop its head off. I can still remember feeling sick to the pit of my stomach at the sight of its body still wriggling. We all screamed and cried, even my tough older brothers.

Not surprisingly, Mom was delighted to have a chicken that Christmas. But as we sat there at the table, Dennis, David and I couldn't help but catch each other's eyes over the juicy piece of meat laid out in front of us. I'm sure we were reliving the experience in our minds of what we'd seen in the courtyard. But we were brought up never to turn our noses up at anything put on the table and besides, I think our appetites soon got the better of us – the meat just looked too good!

11

Painting My Room Pink
and Making the Most of
Cardboard

Dad's first name was Joseph and it suited him right down to the ground – he was a carpenter through and through. I still marvel at his ingenuity when it came to creating absolute masterpieces out of any piece of scrap wood or material he could get his hands on. He had an incredible imagination when it came to transforming everyday items.

By day he worked as a shop steward for Morris Commercial, down Drews Lane. This didn't mean much to me as a little girl; I had no real concept of what he did, but as I understand it now, he would have had responsibility for acting as the labour organisation's local representative and providing information to union leadership. Looking back, this would have suited him down to the ground as he loved organising and taking command. Us kids never really understood the severity of what this meant and it was certainly never discussed with us, but it must have been a stressful time for my parents as it put even more pressure on their finances whenever a strike was in full swing.

Before Morris's, he had worked for Birmingham Small Arms (BSA), where they made guns, pushbikes and, famously, motorbikes. The factory in Small Heath had been used to make small arms during World War II, mainly by women, who worked hard to keep the war supplies going.

I've never seen Dad happier than when he had time alone with his tools, though – sizing up and measuring the wood in front of him, no doubt visualising what it would become – whether a crib for the new baby or a go-kart for the boys. But this hobby also became an invaluable source of income for us too. With an eagle-eye for design he turned old bits of rag into attractive rugs. We were his designated little helpers, of course – we never had time to be bored, our parents always found us a job.

We would visit the neighbours to ask if they had any old clothes to throw out that they hadn't yet given to the rag and bone man. Auntie Lil would also help by lending garments that she'd got cheap from the market. I've always enjoyed art too and later, I'd become a hairdresser, so it was one of the most fun chores to me. I enjoyed sitting there for hours with the older lads, cutting up all the clothes into strips. We'd sort the rags out and put them in separate piles, then Mom and Dad would use a long hooked crochet needle to push the strips through holes in the back and tie them. When the rug was finished, Mom would trim off the surplus. Dad initially started making them just for us but they soon caught the attention of our neighbours and the pub landlord, so the orders came flooding in, which meant a few more coppers towards the housekeeping. These rugs helped to add a touch of individuality to our home too. Dad also made stools of different shapes and sizes for our home, neighbours and the pub. This skill came in quite handy due to the amount of bar stools that got broken during fights in there – he was certainly a pro at spotting a gap in the market!

We constantly battled against the damp in our house. Not only did it smell and pose a potential threat to our health, it meant we couldn't put up wallpaper or lining because nothing would stick. However, Dad came up with a very inventive way to combat this problem that was both decorative and helped our house feel a lot more homely. Quick to find an alternative use for any object, this time it was the dreaded nit comb, normally reserved to scrape the little devils from our curly thick hair. I think the designer Laurence Llewelyn-Bowen might have gasped in admiration at this particular technique – he was a clever guy, my dad! We watched as he got to work, creating a boxed-out wooden panel that ran around the frame of our living room. He didn't explain what he was up to and we knew better than to interrupt him as he pursed his lips in concentration. He then varnished the wood with an orange stain and began to stencil elaborate and intricate patterns with the comb, while it was still wet. Mom was absolutely delighted with the results. He went on to make his own stencils from plywood – birds, zigzags and circles, anything that Mom requested – creating unique designs that lifted some of the doom and gloom of our home.

I felt proud of these individual touches that Dad added and I think it was one of the ways he found to express his love for us, especially because he and Mom weren't able to provide the finer things in life – it can't have been easy. Occasionally I'd crave something that a friend of mine had, who my parents knew was better off. When I was about eight, my friend Carol, who lived on the plusher end of Coventry Road, decorated her entire room in pink wallpaper that was in no danger of peeling off from the damp. It was my favourite colour at the time so I loved it. I chattered on about it to the boys and said, 'Ooh, wouldn't it be nice if the attic was painted pink?' much to their disgust.

Paper, as well as paint, was another scarce commodity in our house and we were always asking people for spare bits. The *Birmingham Argus* or the 'pink 'un', as it was known, on a Saturday was one of my dad's staple treats, along with his smoke and beer. After he had finished with it, it was usually used as fuel for the fire – we'd wrap it up into tight, thin strips for kindling. However, occasionally it served another vital purpose: Dad often took it into the outside toilet to read at great length for hours, the only place he said he could get some peace and quiet. Toilet paper was another rare luxury but I doubt any of the pink 'un's journalists ever envisioned their stories ending up on the backsides of some kids in the slums.

Either way, the 'pink 'un' became yet another indispensable resource in our house to be meted out carefully. So, imagine my surprise when I came home from school a week later – I had the shock of my life to discover that Dad had saved up all his old pink *Argus* newspapers to cover the attic walls. He smiled and said, 'That's just the job, eh? They've covered the walls quite nicely.' I was completely over the moon, beaming away. However, the boys were not so impressed and protested wildly. Dad responded with: 'Yes, I know you've got to sleep in a pink room with your sisters but at least you can keep up with the footie scores!'

But I think the most memorable item he ever made for me was a doll's house. We rarely got a lot for Christmas – normally just an apple, a few nuts, an orange or a doll in our stockings – but that year, Dad put in a huge amount of effort. I often knew if he was knocking up something special because he would sidle off outside to the yard within the little enclosure the council had made to give us some more privacy, but I think he must have also spent many hours working on it when I was in bed.

I was in utter disbelief as I unwrapped it on Christmas morning – it looked just like one of the posh houses in the better parts of the city, a real home with everything I dreamed of owning. It was painted white, with a proper front door that opened, a little carved-out wooden handle that led through to a parlour and a proper kitchen. But I'll never forget the intricate details – the wooden furniture and the red brick roof made from proper thin plywood, with dappled bits of paper stuck on that gave the appearance of tiles. Even the upstairs bedrooms had coloured bits of wallpaper on them. I was thrilled, it was the best Christmas I'd ever had.

In some ways, Dad helped me to visualise my dreams – I used to play with my doll's house pretending it was me living in this lovely big house that looked so warm, inviting and cosy. I'd sit in the attic dreaming of being a mom, taking my kids to the park and owning a string of shops – both of these dreams eventually came true. Although the back-to-backs were tough, they helped me look forward to a better life because it really couldn't ever get any worse!

I was fortunate to have the doll's house all to myself though I sometimes let Barbara play with it – it was rare that I got the chance to have some alone time, up in the attic talking to myself, playing make-believe.

The boys weren't left out either, though. Dad made them the most incredible fort and again, it was the details that he strove to get so right that made it so authentic. As well as a drawbridge that actually opened, he cleverly used the shavings and sawdust left over from the workshop – he sprinkled them on and then dabbed it with green to give the appearance of mould or moss growing on the castle walls. As a finishing decorative touch he used flags from Woolworths. It was this attention to detail that made our gifts so special. Mom also bought cowboy and Indian figures from the market for my brothers to play with.

Dad used his practical skills to help out in our community too. If there was a leaking roof in the middle of winter, he would take on the role of resident dogsbody and be up there fixing it – he wouldn't wait around for somebody from the council to do it. If the rain was pouring in, it was often too much of an emergency anyway. Alan learnt a lot from his practical skills and went on to trade as a roofer once he'd left school.

However, this meant Dad was often landed with some of the worst communal tasks, not least dealing with frozen pipes, a common occurrence in the depths of winter. This was not a job he would have ordinarily volunteered for – who would? But with no twenty-four-hour plumber to call out as part of your annual package, he would be down on his hands and knees, lagging the pipes with old towels to thaw them out. The flush would normally give up at this point too. I think he did it to make our lives that little bit easier, not that dealing with the stench of three other families' waste was any mean feat on a daily basis. In these emergencies the bucket in the outhouse was used as a last resort. If left long enough, its contents would begin to overflow until some poor git – normally my dad – had the pleasure of lugging it over to the drain in the yard to swill out with nothing more hygienic than water. The wonders of communal living, eh? Thank God for Toilet Duck today!

As ever, this weather was particularly hard for the women too, impacting on their chores. Sometimes the stand-pump would freeze in the yard for as long as a few weeks, which meant Mom couldn't wash clothes, sheets or nappies. She'd end up washing them in the scullery sink, although on the odd occasion the tap in there would freeze too. Normally, Dad could fix that quickly enough, though.

Again, no bit of paper was ever wasted. Whenever we had an influx of flies in the summer, Dad stuck 'flypapers' – foot-long strips of paper coated with a sweet-scented but non-setting adhesive – to the light fitting to catch them. This wasn't an attractive sight but we were used to bugs sharing our space and leaving their marks on our ceilings. It seems strange to talk about something so everyday and mundane as cardboard but even now, when I unfold it from packaging or take it out for recycling, I almost think Mom is about to snatch it out of my hands to reuse it – especially in today's consumerist society, where we wear items of clothing for barely a season. It seems unthinkable now that anyone would try to make a pair of shoes last for at least two years to then be handed down to younger siblings, but this was the system in our house.

I only ever had two pair of shoes as a child, one that I wore for everyday – normally a pair of market-bought plimsolls, which I wore to school and ran around in, in all weathers, and then my Sunday best for church. Not surprisingly, over the two years they were constantly wearing down and I would find my feet filling up with water so we used cardboard to help combat this problem.

I still remember my fifth birthday, which was unusually dismal because it was still snowing, even in late March. I'd been really looking forward to it but I knew my friends wouldn't be able to get there if it didn't stop. On the morning of my birthday it was still freezing, and there was thick snow still piling up towards the front door. Mom had put on as good a spread as she always could but by five o'clock when it seemed clear no one was coming, I asked if I could fetch a friend who lived near my school. Yes, it was quite normal for a five-year-old to slip out on their own back then. I was cold, wet and my shoes were soaked through – including the trusty cardboard we relied on – but I was so excited to see my friend that we sled all the way back to Arthur Street.

I envied girls with patent shiny shoes who had their feet measured properly in C&A. It wasn't until I left my junior school to start a new life at Tilton Road Senior School that I left the cardboard behind for good. Here, there was no option but to wear uniform – a navy blue pleated skirt with a matching blazer, complete with the school emblem on the pocket, plus a white blouse. We had to wear black lace-ups or T-bar sensible black shoes too. No more cardboard for me in my old shoes, it was time for brand-new ones.

Mom had to save extremely hard to buy it all, but she thought it was worth every penny when she saw me dressed on my first day. I felt a bit posh and 'above my station' in my uniform but I also thought I was the bee's knees. There were no grants for school uniforms then, but Mom would always find the money somehow.

Dad wasn't a cobbler by trade but he would have a go at everything to help out, including lengthening the life of our shoes. Any bit of leather he acquired was like gold dust, but he would always make the best use of it. He'd cut a mould of the shoe using every inch of its surface to maximise the best possible amount of space once it had worn through. However, as much as we appreciated his efforts, he used nails to fix down the soles – it was excruciatingly painful when they started to cut through! Still, it was a choice between that or soaking wet feet.

So, a good solid pair of durable shoes that lasted a long time, in all weathers, was worth its weight in gold, especially for poor people. The *Daily Mail* newspaper is not to everybody's taste in this country but it did perform a much-needed service with its charitable free boots scheme, particularly in the freezing cold winters. Most kids where we lived owned a pair and there was no stigma attached to this – everyone knew where they'd come from. They were convenient too because once the studs wore away, they could easily be replaced. They also doubled up as proper football boots for those who couldn't afford them or school boots if you took the studs out. Dad applied to the *Daily Mail* for a form to fill in to get the free boots.

Once they'd arrived, he handed them over to Dennis,

declaring that they were '*Daily Mail* boots' and should last him a good time. But they didn't look very attractive to me and I was relieved they were only available to men! They reminded me of big black hobnail boots – stiff, with lots of laces. Of course they were very practical at the time but they appear to be something of a fashion item now, I've noticed. Dad instructed Dennis to 'clean, spit and polish them' so that they could be passed down to David – it was constant hand-me-downs in our house. However, Dennis seemed to find them very painful. Nonetheless, boots were boots and he wore them every single day, come rain or shine.

I came in one day to find my brother soaking his feet in our infamous enamel bowl – we only owned one in the entire house. He had tons of blisters on his feet and was using a pin to burst them. You'll be horrified to know that this enamel bowl served many different purposes in our house – from strip washes to Dad shaving and Mom washing the dishes in it – ugh! After all that, Dad would swill it round under the tap and make pastry in it, for a pie or special treat, such as Manchester Tart. It was actually delicious – he made the pastry from lard, a pinch of salt, and some milk and water. He'd line the meat tin after dinner and cook it in the gas stove. When it was cool, he would spread the pastry (which was hard as old boots!) with jam, then make a custard out of milk and water to pour over the top and wait an hour or two for it to set. We'd have it for tea with jam sandwiches or dripping from the roast at lunchtime. We thought it was great, a nice change from fish paste sandwiches or lard with a pinch of salt on it. Mind you, I'm not sure I'd eat it now out of that enamel bowl, considering all the other activities it was used for!

12

Wash Day in
the Brewus

I absolutely adore my tumble dryer. Honestly, I do! It remains one of my most treasured household items. As I've already said, if it was between that and the dishwasher, I'd choose the tumble dryer any day. There's nothing quite like bringing out my sheets and towels to feel their fluffy warmth against my cheeks. I think my love for this common household object is rooted in memories of our constant battle to get everything dry in the back-to-backs – from our clothes to our sheets. Without modern conveniences we relied on the mercy of good weather or the fire. It wasn't unusual for sheets to be left hanging for days around the fire or strung up on a washing line if it was raining – the damp inside didn't make this any easier either. In particularly cold weather, items were sometimes left hanging outside to freeze-dry in the frost. Us Brits are known for talking non-stop about the weather and not surprisingly, it was one of the main topics of conversation circulating amongst women on a Monday in our court at Arthur Street – wind, breeze and sun were our friends in this weekly battle. But if clouds appeared on the horizon, there would be many a solemn expression from beneath a housewife's tightly wrapped turban plus a few morose exclamations of 'It looks black over Bill's mother's', which meant it was likely to rain. Some think this expression is a reference to William Shakespeare, whose mother – Mary Arden – lived in Stratford-upon-Avon.

Despite our reliance on its fickle nature I still have fond memories of wash day –for the collaborative team spirit it cultivated that you just don't get from sharing a plastic cup of washing powder or lending your neighbour a few spare pegs. Like bath night, washing day was hard, physical work, but everyone was united in the same goal – to clean and dry as many clothes and as much linen as possible. We'd pool all our resources together to achieve this, whether it was sharing out the remains of our Reckitt's blue bag – a powder used to get our whites as white as possible – or lending a spare hand with the mangle handle if Mrs Bottrell looked as though her energy was flagging.

Monday was our designated day, along with Nancy Nee, Mrs Bottrell and Mrs Jeys, which meant the day off school for me to help out. This was fine by me as Monday meant sewing class, which I detested. Needless to say, I can't even sew a button on. Mom felt the same about it and luckily wasn't one to push on this. I, of course, was happy to be off school, and in the long term it has not done my basic education any harm, although I still struggle with spelling – I'm not sure the teachers on a Monday morning could have done much to change that, though. (As well as sewing in the afternoon, there were the three Rs in the morning. I always loved reading – historical romances are still among my favourite books – and I've a natural aptitude for numbers that helped me in all my businesses.)

Our family were due in first to the brewus for ten o'clock. I'm not sure who designated these times for us but Mom and I did our best to ensure we were in there on the dot to get started – time was of the essence.

Mostly it was just me helping out and God, did she need the extra pair of hands, especially when she was pregnant or the babies were very young! For a thin and slight woman her physical strength never failed to amaze me, though looking back, I think she had little choice when faced with the day-to-day slog of each task – it just had to be done. It did take its toll, though. Mom suffered with varicose veins in her later years – nine children and long stints standing at the sausage factory and in the brewus were no doubt contributing factors. Although an extremely attractive woman she aged fast and there are pictures of her in her late fifties and early sixties, where she looks as delicate and frail as an elderly lady. We lost her relatively young at the age of sixty-six. I feel blessed that my life has not been as physically challenging. Occasionally, my older brothers would stay off school to help as well as me, though the only part of the task they relished was starting the fire in the copper brick, which was fundamental to a successful washing day.

Our first task was to carry water from the pump in the yard that we all shared into the brewus. The amenities in here were little changed from the Victorian era but this was one structure that was built to last. They consisted of a copper boiler set in brick, a maiden tub complete with dolly stick, a mangle, washboard and steel iron, identical to the one on our grate. We loved running back and forth collecting water from the pump, but found the galvanised bucket that Mom filled too heavy for us – she'd tell us to get out from under her feet because she had to get the tub in the top filled as quickly as possible, so that the water could start boiling from the fire below. It was just as important to stoke the fire as it was to keep it going so we had to make sure it was topped up with enough fuel throughout.

In the brick was a small opening where we started the fire. It was a similar system to starting the fire in our grate. We arranged strips of paper at the bottom, then chopped-up pieces of wood and finally, balanced the coal on top. We loved to watch the fire start roaring in the furnace and wait for the water to begin bubbling and boiling away on top. On a freezing cold day it was one of our favourite places to be as it was lovely and warm in there. In the summer of course it was the opposite – we were extremely hot and would soon start flagging under the weight of the task. Dad placed one of the stools he made in there so that we could each take rests in between keeping the fire stoked. There was constant pressure on to do this because if a fire went out, it not only wasted time but also meant the next neighbour in after us would have to start it up again.

Once the water was boiling, the sheets would go in first because Mom wanted to get them as white as possible. The majority of our sheets were old, thin and tearing, so our feet were constantly tearing holes in them. But they'd always be the whitest whites flying in the breeze of the courtyard, determined to shine even under the weight of the smog and fog. For the washing powder we'd grate soap into the tub of boiling water then add a blue bag of powder to get the sheets as white as possible. The brand Mom used was Reckitt's. Before the dawn of laundry detergents this was stirred into the final rinse and in its earlier day had names like stone blue, fig blue or thumb blue. We knew it as Reckitt's Blue or dolly bags. The main ingredients were synthetic ultramarine and baking soda, and the original squares weighed an ounce. I never knew all this at the time, I just thought it was magic. (You can still buy it, as Reckitt's Crown Blue, in paper-wrapped cubes.)

After the sheets had been boiled up in the brick, I'd transfer them to the rectangular-shaped galvanised steel maiden tub with wooden tongs – absolutely essential to avoid scorching our hands! We added in some of the hot water from the boiler, where washing would continue by hand with the help of the wooden dolly stick – it was about a hundred centimetres in height and had a crossways handle for extra grip at the top, with six legs circulating out of the base.

It was a tough process, especially when I was small, to swirl and twist the sheets and clothes in there. But as with so many of these chores I can't remember being taught or shown – like handling the draw tin, you just picked these things up as you went along, though I do remember Mom looking on in despair a few times at my method – 'God, we'll be here all day at your rate, Maureen!' Mom treated a dolly the way she treated all other household objects – as a means to getting something accomplished quickly and speedily, before moving on to the next task. She complained of us kids getting under her feet but deep down I think she did appreciate our help, although it was always just a given that we would.

In the maiden tub I scrubbed shirt collars and cuffs on the washboard, which contained a panel made of corrugated zinc. This item hadn't evolved on much further from the Victorian Age either. Sometimes it was difficult not to tip water out over the edges of the tub if I was particularly vigorous! I also used a brush for extra scrubbing – tough work, but the end was by no means in sight. After rinsing under the cold tap I had the mangle to contend with next. It was a steel-framed hand operated machine with two rotating wooden rollers for squeezing out all the excess water. If any of the clothes had buttons I had to be careful how I arranged them so that they didn't crack during the process. Some of our neighbours were so diligent they would even remove the buttons each time but this was a tedious practice that, not surprisingly, never appealed to Mom or me! Our fingers were more precious than buttons though, which I learnt quickly from a young age when I nearly squashed a couple in the rollers.

The mangle was heavy and worn and had somehow survived about a hundred years of use. If we put sheets through, Mom would hold one end and I would hold the other. We'd fold them, put them in the mangle and wring them as tight as possible. Then we would use the first line in the yard and peg them out to dry if, hope to God, it wasn't raining. Next in the garment pecking order were our everyday clothes, which included our school uniforms. We'd rinse them in cold, clean water and put them through the mangle too. Then it was our underwear. Finally, it was Dad's overalls, which he used for work or woodcarving. If we were lucky enough to get all these items dry, I would take turns with Mom to iron them – the iron would have been kept on the fire earlier to get it very hot. I always needed a cloth to hold it – there were no plastic tops or handles in those days, at least not in the back-to-backs, and after burning your hand, you would soon learn. Perhaps this is why I hate ironing so much. However, it would soon get cold so you had to return it to the fire. Finally, our clothes would be given a final airing outdoors in the breeze and then warmed around the hearth with the sheets, where they would billow peacefully, like flags sailing into shore.

In between the frantic rush to be out by twelve, Mom found time to have a quick gossip or moan with Lily Jeys, or Nancy Nee, who shared the same brewus. One of them would wait for their shift, which was normally between one and three in the afternoon. I'd pretend to be busy mangling of course but would strain my ears to catch what I could here and there – they kept hushed tones but it was normally a customary groan regarding the weather, their kids, but most of all, their 'old man' as they called their husbands. More often than not, they'd had too much to drink in the pub the night before and had kept their wife up all night with 'a bad tummy' or a bout of coughing. Occasionally, I'd catch snippets of conversation concerning the dreaded 'moonlit flit' so I knew some poor sod was in trouble with the rent man or law – thankfully, it was never us.

When Mom was incredibly busy on wash day it was difficult to pay much attention to the babies. When Stephen and Philip were little they'd sleep in the pram outside the brewus – one at the top, the other at the bottom. That way I could help with washing while the kids were safe asleep, not under our feet or crying. Of course, if they weren't asleep, they'd usually be crying so sometimes Mom would do a bottle for them or change their nappy halfway through. Or I'd push them around the yard in the pram. Once they were asleep, I would continue with Monday's chores. Mom was convinced the fresh air did them good anyway and I think she was right – many a time they would sit happily in the pram with a bottle or a rusk, happy as Larry while we got on with the tasks in hand.

Even the persistent smell of drainage that hung in the air was drowned out by wafts of boiled carbolic soap and dolly bags. It was hard work but I felt a great sense of satisfaction as I climbed into bed every Monday night, happy to breathe in the smell of fresh clean laundry. I'd certainly never swap it for my tumble dryer again though, that's for sure!

13

Bombsites and Collecting Fuel for Bonfire Night

Bonfire Night was one of the most important dates in the calendar for us, bringing light and sparkle to the cold, dark months in the back-to-backs. It seems hard to believe that we could buy fireworks when we were kids – it's now an offence to sell them to anyone under eighteen. Of course, we need to keep our children safe but it seems a shame they're so far removed from the experience now – standing hundreds of feet away, watching communal displays in some park, or twirling a few sparklers in the garden under the watchful eye of their parents. Us kids loved organising the night in our courtyard, and in fact we were actively encouraged to take the lead in its planning and preparation, and were determined to make the biggest and best bonfire we could in the whole neighbourhood.

We didn't take much notice of the politics behind the night, of course – Guy Fawkes was just some mischievous bloke who tried to blow up Parliament many years ago, but my brothers and I pulled together all the resources we could to construct our guy from any old clothes and rags we could get our hands on, in and around the neighbourhood. We stuffed old trousers and jumpers with scrunched-up paper or old laddered stockings of Mom's and made a mask tied on with string and an old hat. By the time we'd finished he looked almost human – so convincing was his body shape and in the run-up to the night, we began to feel as though he was another member of the family.

Dennis and David were particularly good at creating lifelike figures – although there were times when they used this skill to perform one of their more mischievous, albeit darker pranks. Of course, they loved to egg each other on, but this went a bit too far once when they ended up terrifying Old Gal Griffey – Mrs Griffin. Dennis had a guitar that he'd bought on sale in the pawn shop – he saved up hard to buy it and used to play it and sing to us in the yard. He thought he was Arthur Street's answer to Tommy Steele, I think. One evening, the boys dressed it up in school uniform – old grey socks, trousers and a jumper. As ever, they were very imaginative with whatever resources were available: they used wool for hair that they coloured black with polish and even painted a face on. Then they got some rope and tied him round the neck of the guitar to hang out of the window of the attic. Poor Old

Gal Griffey came running out, shouting and crying for my parents to call an ambulance, while Dennis and David fell about laughing upstairs on the floor. Dad was furious of course and gave them a good hiding, not that that would ever stop them – Dennis just loved encouraging dark horse David to come up with more twisted ideas.

Some of my happiest memories are taking the guy into the centre of town, pulling him along on one of our homemade carts made out of an old pram and planks of wood. We'd make our way along Coventry Road and sit outside Woolworths and the butcher's shop squawking 'Penny for the guy!' We've all got good business sense in our family – perhaps because the importance of raising cash was instilled in us so young. Sometimes we made up to three shillings (15p; about £2.50 now) and got a real buzz from investing it back into treats for the night – potatoes, chestnuts, plus sweets and pop to share around the whole family. We also bought jumping jacks, Roman candles, Catherine wheels and bangers. It's pretty self-explanatory what they did – they weren't that dissimilar to a stick of dynamite and, not surprisingly, are now banned. The fact we contributed all this cash towards the night really helped out Mom and I think it boosted our confidence too, making us realise what we were capable of. But we put the most amount of effort into collecting resources for our masterpiece of the evening – the bonfire. As with the snowmen in winter, we were determined to have the biggest and the best on our street – the stakes were high so our competitive streak came out in all its blazing glory. We started planning and preparing as early as the end of the summer, gathering whatever we could, already envisioning our towering inferno in the courtyard. We scavenged for wood on the bombsites behind the bus depot at the end of our road, knocked on neighbours' doors and pleaded for old bits of furniture. We'd hunt down old newspapers and cardboard boxes too.

Laughing and tired but always happy in our quest, we'd head to the market, gathering more dirt as the days went on. People sometimes gave us odd looks as though we'd jumped out of the Victorian era but we didn't care, we just stayed focused on the job.

The barrow boys in the market were always generous and gave us any of their leftover wooden boxes and crates. But this was already part of everyday life: we were always down the bombsites searching for whatever scraps we could, from the tyres off wheels to turn into a hula hoop to cardboard for our shoes.

During World War II, Birmingham was bombed more than any other British city after London. Altogether 100,000 houses were destroyed or damaged, some of which were down the back of our street. Occasionally, we'd dig up pennies, a tin hat or even the odd piece of gold – we'd beam with pride as we presented our wares to Mom and Dad, who'd say, 'Ta, loves, stick it over there on the side.' Sometimes they were really pleased with what we brought back, though – Dad used to sell on any pipes we found. We'd store the wood we found in the cellar to dry out. It was a great backup if we ran out of coal, but at this time of year it was essential fuel for our bonfire too.

It wasn't easy to keep everything we collected dry or to get it all home. If the wind was strong, I was often chasing after bits of paper and cardboard down the streets – our precious wares! We would store a lot of it in our yard, jammed into the sheds or down the cellar for the weeks ahead, or even the brewus. The old ladies would moan and say, 'Get it out, we have to get our washing done,' but we wanted to keep it dry and safe from other kids nicking stuff off our turf for their own bonfires! This was war and we had worked hard. Mom and Dad would moan too but also understood it was a special one-off night that brought everyone together into the yard.

The night before we were often so overcome with excitement we'd have to release our pent-up energy somehow. It was tradition to play 'Knock, Knock, Run', much to the fury of our neighbours, and keep an eye out for any last-minute thieves who might be after our produce.

We stacked up bonfires that reached heights of twenty-odd feet and spread out at least ten feet across. Piles and piles of wood, furniture, doors or other combustibles, and any bits of old domestic rubbish that people had thrown out. Health and Safety regulations would never allow it now.

There were no ladders to help us get to the top either – just plenty of enthusiasm, persistence and clambering involved! We got a lot of cuts and bruises and would often narrowly miss the odd bit of falling furniture. I'll never forget the looks on the faces of the kids in the other yards as they saw the size of our bonfire – every year we'd aim to build it higher than the one before.

Dad and Mom always marvelled at how much we got in, year in, year out, and looked really proud when some of the neighbours said it was the biggest bonfire they'd ever seen. There was one year when we thought we would have to call the Fire Brigade – it was so big that it nearly got out of control. But it was always a shame to see our guy go up in smoke. We'd grown attached to him over the week, as he accompanied us on our expeditions. So it was with a mix of sadness and delight that we'd finally place him upon the wooden pyre. Dad supervised Dennis and David as they took a match to a rolled-up newspaper and walked around, lighting it on all sides. I loved to feel the intense heat of the flames on my face as they reached higher and higher.

And miraculously, the rain always seemed to hold out on Bonfire Night. I never remember it dampening the night's proceedings, not once. It was a night when we were always allowed to stay up late too, into the early hours, even if we had school the next day – we wouldn't have been able to sleep anyway.

We were far too excited to ever get cold and we were so used to freezing temperatures anyway, but if the warmth of the blazing fire wasn't enough then we drank tins of hot potato soup or baked a potato in the ashes of the fire. Nancy Nee made tea and hot chocolate for us all and kept telling us not to get too close. 'You'll end up like Guy Fawkes and I ain't being doctor tonight, I've had too much to drink,' she warned.

Dad and his friends would come back from the pub with fresh jugs of ale, while the women drank whisky, gin or just settled for a cup of tea and a roaring fire they hadn't had to struggle to make for a change!

If Bonfire Night fell well before bath night we reeked of smoke and fireworks for days, but we didn't care. We danced around the fire, singing at the tops of our voices: 'Bonfire Night, we all have a fight to little angels dressed in white'. Yes, we were all little angels until the fire needed stoking. I'm still sworn to secrecy regarding the legend of Old Gal Griffin's chair that sadly perished in one of our bonfires. Wouldn't you know, she'd only been nestling in it happily, resting her bad legs, with a hot cocoa all but five minutes before. Up she went to use the lav and returned to find it long gone – some rogue had chucked it in to stoke the fire. 'Where's my bloody chair gone?' she ranted. No one wanted to get the sharp end of her boiler stick so the culprit had already scarpered down the entry – in defence, I don't think they'd done it on purpose!

14

Freezing Cold Winters, Fog and Smog and Joey Ellis's Magic Wand

Aside from freezing cold temperatures, our winters were plagued by another enemy that hung in swathes around us, clouding our vision and weighing down our spirits as well as our lungs. With smokeless fuel and cleaner exhausts as common as they are now, it seems strange to think that smoke and fog ever had such an impact. But it was a reality for us that brought a whole new meaning to the Christmas carol 'In the Bleak Midwinter'.

Fortunately, some Members of Parliament were taking this issue seriously. In 1950, Mr F. Longden, MP for Birmingham Small Heath, raised it in Parliament, stating the 'very fearful legacy' of the factory system. In his speech regarding smoke abatement he states that there are 6,000 factories with more than 24,000 chimney stacks 'every one of which is an active or potential emitter of poisonous, noxious fumes, dirt, filth and slag'. This is what we had to contend with on a daily basis. We were breathing in grit, ash, soot and tar filled with all sorts of harmful deposits such as sulphates, chlorides, calcium and sodium salts. Longden estimated that at least 60 per cent of the pollution was from industrial sources, with the remainder from commercial and domestic sources. They contributed to some particularly miserable winters, where we were often walking in snow as deep as six inches. Us kids hated it because there were times when it got so bad that we had to stay in. The streets were no longer ours to play in – they belonged to these noxious substances. We were confined to the gloom of the attic, which had even less light coming in from our small window anyway. The damp and cold seemed to seep through to our bones with greater strength.

When we had to go out to school, it would take us twice as long to get there – most kids were late, even our teachers. Sometimes Dad couldn't get to work at the car factory if there was too little visibility for the buses to get through – 'no work, no pay' was the rule then.

Mom walked to the sausage factory on the Coventry Road. She would be freezing cold and wet by the time she got there, but she would make it in all weathers. Often she'd be exhausted too, up all night nursing the little 'uns suffering from rheumatic fever. These illnesses could be potentially very serious. As Longden also stated in his speech, the effects of the smog could even result in deaths, the majority of which were related to respiratory illnesses that included pneumonia and bronchitis.

Mom detested this time of year, understandably – it made the daily stresses of getting by even harder, the extra pressure to find coke or slack if our coal supply ran out. I don't know how she coped with the endless stream of sheets and nappies she needed to get dry either.

The fog scared me and I tried not to go out in it all. The air was weighed down with a heavy silence, just as we were. All around were huddling figures, wrapped in shawls, desperate to get out of the fog as quickly as possible. There was no time for any chatter. The atmosphere was full of tension and aggression – horns tooting, men shouting obscenities and the plaintive sound of babies crying. If you heard a scream or a bang, it normally meant someone had bumped into a car or a lamp post. No sounds at all though were even eerier.

For my brothers, it was a chance to cause extra mischief, though – they delighted in scaring the wits out of me, Ann and Valerie whenever they could. At points it got so cloudy down Arthur Street we could barely see our hands in front of our faces. The lads would leap out on us or drift behind us, shouting boo and banging on bins. Their favourite trick was telling us to watch for the car creeping down the road. However, we never believed them because they were always playing tricks so on the odd occasion it was actually true, we'd walk into the back of a car crawling along the street. The few that did come down our road often ended up wrapped around a lamp post or rammed up the back of another. Most of the time they would crawl, but you would get the odd idiot who even sped down there.

In the distance I could hear buses chugging down Coventry Road – the busiest road in Birmingham, it suffered many accidents during this time. Sometimes the bus conductor would walk in front of the bus when it was particularly bad. I saw this on my way to the moneylender's house one day – I used to clutch the money she lent us inside my mitten because if I dropped it, I would never find it again in the fog. Woe betide me if I did! I think the most I ever lost was a ten-shilling note (50p, but equivalent to about £8 in today's money). The fog also made my hair and clothes wet and damp, but there was little we could do other than sit in them all day. For me this was an extra pain because of my hair. It would bunch up into tight curls and matt together – impossible to comb and get the tangles out at the end of the day.

I used to long for the busy roar of traffic again down Coventry Road as a sign we'd won the battle against this bleak blanket that hung over us. I still counted my blessings though and thanked my lucky stars I wasn't blind or partially sighted – I could at least see, if only a foot in front of myself.

We would regularly come down with coughs and colds during those winters. Mom was normally too busy tending to the littler children who were ill, so it was quite common for me, Alan, Dennis and David to all be in bed at the same time – this was particularly unbearable because it meant we were all coughing and spluttering over each other, spreading the germs! We didn't have tissues or a muslin either – we would pass round and share old bits of rag and small hankies if we were lucky. As you can imagine they were soon soaked through.

Mom would make us swallow down some brown cough mixture from the doctor's, which tasted disgusting, but we all had to have it as daily medicine even when we weren't ill – prevention is better than cure, as she would say. If Dad was ill, he'd go to bed with warm milk and whisky. It sounds like an old wives' tale but even now I still find it's one of the best cures. Mom would just battle on if she was ill – we'd help where we could, but I've no idea where she got the energy from. It was rare to hear her complain – like most women of her day, she just got on with what she could and took it all in her stride. It was also rare for Dad to take to his bed. Because money was our lifeline, he had to go to work, like it or not – in those days, you had to be very ill to miss work.

Barbara and I wore scarves around our faces to offer protection when we went out. On their way to school the boys wore one of Auntie Lil's balaclavas or a pair of mittens she'd knitted, but they would get so damp that there was no point wearing them home – there was no facility on the school premises to dry them out during the day anyway. We had a lost property box that was always full of hats, balaclavas, mittens and odd socks – if we lost anything, we would often poach items from there because parents never sewed names into them as is common today and couldn't afford to replace them. During these freezing spells, we still had to do PE in our vests and knickers!

To add to this, we often had severe snow storms and freezing temperatures, which contributed to our misery. These poor weather conditions meant that the schools and factories were often closed. We didn't mind missing school of course but it was miserable for the working classes, who were usually laid off. We heard Dad talk to Mom about food and fuel supplies that were stranded in the docks. To add to the misery, wages were reduced and it was the norm to go hungry.

We used to help the elderly people in our community too, during these bleak winters, by clearing the snow from their doors. Though they were tough and used to these conditions, it seemed unfair that they were isolated even more. They were also trapped by the housing situation because there was no reason for the council to move them (for example, having children over a particular age or a serious illness), so they tended to be marooned in the same situation.

As if that wasn't enough, when the roads did begin to thaw, this would cause severe flooding. And as you might imagine this weather put a further strain on our insufficient and basic sanitary conditions. Our gazunda (so-called because it goes under the bed) or po (short for 'chamber pot') was made of porcelain. It was essential in the nights when it was too cold to venture outside. However, in the dreadful winters it was often stretched to breaking point with all four of us using it in the night so we had to transfer the contents to a bucket on the tiny landing or use that if one of us had particularly bad diarrhoea or was throwing up because of a stomach bug. The contents were then taken out the next morning to throw down the drain in the yard and swill under the outdoor pump. Not surprisingly, none of us leapt at the chance to drag a heavy bucket of slops out – any arguments over who this horrible task befell were normally cut short anyway by Mom or Dad shouting their objections up the stairs to us, at the stench that was finding its way into their bedroom.

This was if the bucket hadn't already been kicked over in the night – also a regular occurrence as we were normally stumbling around in the dark. It was difficult to know what was worse – mopping up all the slops with little more than a floor cloth or facing our parents' anger if this happened. It's where the expression 'kick the bucket' comes from because you were liable to get killed if you were responsible for this. Despite our lack of any decent indoor plumbing – a wonderful blessing that we all take for granted nowadays – Mom was determined to keep the house as clean, sanitary and fresh-smelling as possible. She removed any rubbish from the house into the miskins as quickly as possible, not just because of the smell, but because there was nowhere to properly store it.

Dad was also ahead of his time in that he made a small

cupboard for storing any unused or potentially reusable items – now of course, it's called recycling.

Mom did her best to combat unpleasant smells in our house with carbolic soap or cardinal polish, but she resorted to more traditional methods too. We used to make our own perfume from the wild roses in Auntie Lil's garden – we'd pick the petals and shake them in a bottle of water (left in the bottle, however, our perfume would go black and very smelly). The grass at the bottom of her long garden was so high that when we played down there, you could hardly see us.

Having said that, in amongst some of the worst smells – the po, the boys' smelly feet or the wee that stained the sheets in the night – there are smells from my childhood that I remember fondly. There's nothing quite like the smell of an open, real coal fire to take me back to breakfasts in front of our fireplace, nibbling at jam on toast we'd singed in the flames with a long-pronged fork.

It brought a tear to my eye when I visited the restored back-to-backs and saw the tiny attic room, no bigger than two by three metres across – it was so reminiscent of the early years I spent sleeping in the same bed as my brothers. Most people I knew shared beds with their siblings – ours was three-quarter size (about three by four feet across), slightly bigger than an average single. Our bedtime routine was usually a noisy ritual with the four of us – Dennis, me, Alan and David – angling for our share of the sheet or blanket, struggling to get warm when it was cold. Feet in your face, arms and legs everywhere, as well as a kick or two from one just as you were drifting off to sleep.

The sheets were thin and fragile from washing and boiling them so they would tear easily where we pulled them back and forth – Mom hated sewing so much that mending them was usually the last chore on the list! However, we did all have our own pillows. There weren't any pillowcases on them, but they were stuffed with flock, a type of old cloth torn to pieces.

Dennis loved to tell a good yarn and would keep us awake with hilarious stories, which made the humdrum and tediousness of bedtime easier. In particular, he kept us amused for hours with his tales of an imaginary figure called Joey Ellis, who he pretended was one of the Ellises adopted sons. Unbeknownst to his parents, Joey had magical powers from a ring he wore at all times that his real family had given him. If he rubbed the ring, he could be transported anywhere or make anything happen – he'd get us in the pictures for free, to football matches at The Blues or fetch us ice cream, sweets and fish and chips, as well as give us warm coats and all the bikes or toys we wanted. Often Dennis would spin these yarns at night so we'd work up a real appetite before bedtime.

Joey was like Father Christmas – even on a cold, miserable and foggy night, which we frequently experienced, he'd transport us to another hot country. He'd make anyone happy or grant any request and could even fly like Peter Pan. Dennis would draw us into these stories, where we were treated like kings and queens – we'd beg him to tell us more before we fell asleep dreaming that all these wonders would come true in the morning. And we were all sworn to secrecy. For us these stories livened up cold and miserable nights as we lay huddled together. I remember often looking up at the moon and stars shining through the small window in our attic before we fell asleep, happy, safe and warm.

Of course, looking back, it's not difficult to see the wish fulfilment lurking within the subtext of these stories – we were craving better lives and Joey made that possible. I often think that Dennis would have liked to be the Joey figure, snapping his fingers and magically materialising our hopes and wishes. Somewhere deep down, he must have felt responsible for our emotional as well as our physical day-to-day needs – he couldn't put it into words directly to us though, except through these stories. As an adult, I can put it all into context and realise the pressure this put him under.

I recently remembered how Dennis used to sleepwalk. We found it quite funny at the time of course, especially when he'd kick the bucket full of slop over on the landing. One winter night, he even went so far as walking out in the snow, down Arthur Street, and bumping into a lamp post. Sometimes he would come back with a bruised or black eye without realising he'd been up the street and back! He just thought he had a nose bleed until he did the same thing the next night and one of the neighbours picked him up and brought him back. Mom had to soak the bed clothes and his pyjamas in cold water with salt. They took him to the doctor's but it was never discussed with us kids, of course. I do remember that we were told to just guide him back to bed though whenever it happened because it was dangerous to wake him – I can't remember how old we were when this started but I do remember now that it happened fairly regularly. After we moved to Sheldon, however, Dennis's sleepwalking stopped. I have no idea why.

15

Polio and a Convalescence Trip to Devon

I've been blessed to go on some wonderful holidays in my lifetime. Even to places that may as well have been on another planet, when I saw them on the black and white reels on Pathé News. This was when the most exotic holiday I knew of anyone in my family having was Uncle Ray's trip to Spain at some time in the late 1950s or early 1960s. And even a trip to stay at Auntie Phoebe's or Auntie Lil's felt like a luxury spa break. But as an adult, I've even fulfilled my childhood dream of being a Hawaiian girl – well, sort of, I still haven't quite mastered the hula! However, I can honestly say that if you offered me the choice of a trip to the Seychelles, a Caribbean cruise or back to the farm I stayed on in Devon many years ago, I would choose the latter. I could be lying under a palm tree, rocking gently in a hammock, receiving a five-star massage with every whim or need catered for and it still wouldn't compare to the hospitality and kindness I revelled in that week as an eight-year-old.

Of course, there is the minor issue of the time machine I'd need to transport me back too because it was the people on that farm who made it so special – in particular, the farmer's wife. Despite this, I can't remember her name or where we stayed in Devon; neither have I been able to track down its whereabouts in recent years. But the image of her as the healthy and hearty farmer's wife, embodying all that's wholesome and good about life on a farm has crystallised in my mind. It's almost as though Ma from *The Darling Buds of May* was styled on her – with her red and ruddy cheeks, a complexion that perpetually glowed from the kiss of the sun and the sting of fresh country air, she had wavy silver-grey hair that crowned her smiling face. And she was never without her crisp starch apron that wrinkled up around her generously plump frame either.

She is a figure from childhood that has remained very vivid to me over the decades for the wonderful way she left me feeling. I don't think I've ever felt such gentleness, tenderness and respect from anyone. It was the seemingly little things that touched me – like offering me pieces of raw carrot, brushing my hair before bed or handing me a towel before I hopped out of the bath. I left that week feeling as though I was the most spoilt child on earth and I think I remember her still all these years later because she embodies the difference that little kindnesses can make: it's a feeling that money can't buy. However, those wonderful memories are tinged with sadness, as are the events leading up to my holiday there. It was only possible because of the cruel hand of fate that my friend Eileen had been dealt. Had we been born all but five years later, the opportunity may never have presented itself.

Thankfully it's rare to see any child in the UK struck down with the debilitating diseases that affected so many of my generation in the post-war years. Welsh Labour minister Aneurin Bevan's drive to make welfare available for all had improved health overall – the high levels of vitamins A and D in cod-liver oil substituted meagre diets that were lacking in nutrition, while orange juice helped to prevent scurvy. But when I was growing up, it was still not an uncommon sight to see a child with skeletal deformities caused by rickets. And poor sanitation meant at least one of us kids was ill every month with disease and ailments that were common to back-to-back living – bronchitis, impetigo or just the common cold. But it was polio that struck fear into the hearts of many a community, not least because it seemed so strange, inexplicable and shrouded in mystery.

And it was merciless in its choice of victim, attacking the most vulnerable in society – babies and children. No one really knew when or where it would strike next. Perhaps this is why our families and society at large seemed so reluctant to ever talk about it openly – you can't explain what you can't understand. It was yet another subject that got swept under the carpet.

It's strange to think that all but sixty years ago people were paralysed by polio – 8,000 every year, in fact. If you were lucky you might learn to walk again, but tragically, 5–10 per cent even died after their breathing muscles became immobilised. The iron lung was a bizarre and terrifying contraption that looked as horrible as it sounded – a mechanical respirator for poor souls who'd been robbed of the energy and capacity to breathe. And to add to the further cruelty of this disease was the fact that it was highly contagious. Children couldn't even receive comforting hugs and cuddles from relatives in the early months, so they were shut off even further, which must have compounded any feelings of shame or the fear it was somehow their fault.

We were very fortunate that none of us caught the virus in our family. Interestingly, there is a theory that the more exposed you are to different viruses and bacteria, the less likely you are to catch it, so there's the possibility our upbringing in the back-to-backs may have served us well in that capacity. The more affluent children often seemed to fall prey to it, perhaps because they hadn't built up an immunity – there's a high chance we may have had the symptoms, but were able to fight them off. We battled many other diseases, such as scarlet fever and yellow fever, as well as the more common ones that still exist today – chicken pox and measles.

Fortunately for us, there was a clever bloke in the US called Jonas Salk, who persevered in finding a vaccine. By 1955, it was in widespread use. I can still remember us all queuing up for the injection. We'd hear the yelps and cries from the victims before us – little comfort, of course. I came to envy the kids later on in the early sixties who enjoyed the perks of the oral vaccine – they were lucky enough to get a lump of sugar!

I'd had injections before, of course. TB was the most memorable – my dad took me along to the doctor for that one – many people of my generation have the signature round scar somewhere on their body. It hurt, but I remember Dad saying, 'It's better than having TB!' He was right of course, and would know, what with Mom losing both parents to the disease. Other than that, we didn't really have the time to go to the doctor's because it meant taking a day off. Nurses at the welfare centre would barely look at you either, unless they saw something of serious concern – they were more preoccupied with the babies or younger children. However, when I queued up for the polio jab I had a very different attitude. I'd witnessed first-hand the damage this cruel disease could cause. I knew it would be painful but nothing compared to the plight of my close friend.

Eileen lived on the opposite side of our yard. There weren't many other kids up that end, though – 'Get up yer own end!' was a slur often hurled at us whenever we ventured out of our own perimeters. So, Eileen would play out with us and I remember her being something of a tomboy like me. But all that changed when she contracted the disease.

Once struck down with it, she was confined to her house most of the time in between visits to the hospital. Previously a happy and active girl, she became a shadow of her former self. But I was entrusted with the task of visiting Eileen to 'cheer her up' when she was out of quarantine. At the time, I still had no concept of the extent of her illness. I'd asked Mom if it was OK to see her and she replied: 'Yes, I think she will be glad to see you, she's been having a bit of a bad time lately.' This was something of an understatement, of course but I didn't press her for more information, as I suspected my questions wouldn't be answered. The secrecy and silence surrounding this disease seemed to add to its misery too.

As I was going out, she told me to wash my face and hands, change into a dress and comb my hair, which I always hated because it hurt when Mom tried to get the tangles – or 'lugs', as we called them – out. She then tied my hair up in a red ribbon, like a chocolate box. I thought it was rather a lot of fuss just to visit a friend, who wouldn't care what I looked like – I felt a bit too posh and dressed up like a dog's dinner.

As was the norm in our neighbourhood, Eileen's door was unlocked. I walked in to find her sitting in a chair, her shoulder-length fair hair propped up against the pillows by the fire. I was shocked to see her legs wrapped in thick white bandages and iron straps that went all the way down to her feet. Unable to conceal my alarm, I said, 'Oh my God, what have you got on your legs?' She replied that the doctor at the hospital had told her to wear them and that she had to drink horrible medicine and tablets – even worse than cod-liver oil.

This was before vaccinations were commonplace so it's likely these unpleasant potions would have antitoxin in them, which was used to block access to nerve cells. She may also have been injected with serum or a lumbar puncture. I felt so sorry for her as she looked at me sadly and said the words that nobody from my generation ever wanted to say: 'I have polio.'

Although I'd now seen the physical effects of this disease first-hand, I still couldn't take it all in. What did this mean? How long would she be ill? When could she take the terrible iron straps off? I was shocked when she said it would take a long time for her to heal, that she wouldn't be able to walk for a long time and would need exercise to learn to walk all over again. She had to wear the irons for support and to help her get stronger.

It was awful to see my friend in so much pain. As much as we were the 'dead-end kids', we made our own entertainment on the streets and had a lot of fun – it seemed so unfair that Eileen was missing out. I gave her a hug and kissed her cheek. However, I kept my head away from hers, just in case she had nits. Mom always warned me not to get too near in case people are unwell or in hospital, as that's where nits tend to breed.

Feeling sorry for my mate was one thing but catching nits again was quite another. Funny really, at that moment it seemed an even worse prospect than contracting polio!

I started visiting Eileen on a regular basis. As a notorious chatterbox I was constantly told off at school, but now I was allowed to talk until the cows came home but for once it seemed to help – and no one threatened me with the ruler! I kept Eileen amused with stories of my siblings' escapades. Although they drove me mad in their various quests to scare me half to death – creeping up on me during a 'lick and a promise' in the scullery or chucking jumping jacks down the entry while I was walking down it, she loved to hear how David had trapped his fingers in the grate yet again and more. She was an only child, so she enjoyed hearing what we'd all been up to – it helped her feel a part of it all still. I made quite a fuss of her when I saw her too, bringing her round an apple we'd pinched while scrumping or some bluebells we'd picked from Chelmsley Wood. Her mom would glance over and say, 'It makes me so happy to see her laugh.' I don't think I ever fully realised the extent of her illness though and what she had to cope with.

A few weeks later, after I'd first visited Eileen, Mom said she'd been chatting to her mom. The doctor thought that a couple of weeks in the country convalescing would do her the world of good because she needed some fresh air and good food to build her up. I asked Mom what 'convalescing' meant and she said it's when you need a rest away for a while to build you up and make you stronger and better. It was like a holiday or a tonic, she told me.

I remembered that she'd gone away on a trip when I was younger, and we'd all been shipped off to various aunts. Mom had been able to do this by paying into an insurance scheme called the Saturday Fund – so-called because people paid into it on a Saturday, after they had received their wages, which were always given cash in hand on a Friday. Mom organised it through the club man and paid three pennies a week for it. Over the years this had helped her take some time out when the exhaustion of raising seven children and the demands of juggling both work and home became too much. Of course, none of us ever knew the real reasons why she went away – it was perhaps three or four times in my childhood memory. I've no doubt it was linked to the strain of having a child almost every year for ten years and never having the chance to properly recuperate.

It was also the Saturday Fund that helped pay for Eileen's trip – and I bless the doctor who suggested it because I think that one week in the Devonshire air helped compensate for a little of the pain she experienced. And I'm so grateful and forever in her debt that her mom chose me to go with her. When they first told Eileen, she cried and said she would hate being all alone and it would make her feel worse, so her mom suggested I go with her. Mom agreed that I could, if the Saturday Fund would cover my expenses.

I was so excited – I had never been to the country before and we were going to stay on a farm. I was a little apprehensive about what clothes to take with me, though. What did people even wear on a farm? David had a pair of wellies that were a size too big for me but I hoped no one but me would notice how lost I was in them. I also took two pairs of his grey, knee-length woolly school socks because I hadn't any of my own.

Although the Saturday Fund covered my expenses it was back to the pawn shop again to cover the cost of some more clothes for me, so that I didn't show my family up when I was down on the farm. They'd be second-hand of course, but we could never afford brand new. Mom took Dad's trusty suit in, as well as an old clock that spent more time in there than it ever did at our house – I'm not convinced it ever told the correct time anyway, what with David constantly fiddling with it.

As ever, our very own dressmaker, Auntie Lil, came to the rescue. She took me to the rag market in the Bull Ring to rifle through the stalls. We had a great time choosing – she bought a couple of pairs of knickers, vests, socks and shoes, as well as a couple of dresses. They were too big for me but her trick was always to turn them up to allow for growth into the next year. When she put new buttons on and worked her magic they looked as good as anything from C&A.

She even knitted me a new jumper with all the spare bits of wool she had left over – all different shades of the rainbow. It's rare to see young people with hankies now, you'll normally only ever see people from my generation with them tucked up their sleeves. An old bit of rag had many uses in our house and this was only one of them. But Mom and Auntie Lil weren't happy about me using this as a substitute for my trip down the farm. Magically, Lil pulled some cotton white hankies edged with lace from out of her big dressing-up box – she swilled them out, ironed them dry and folded them away for me to use.

I asked her why I couldn't just use the old bits of rag that we always used and she said, 'Because we don't want you showing us up.' Not before adding: 'Don't forget to blow your nose on them, not your sleeve!'

I wondered how long I was going for with the amount of things that were packed in the old battered case. It was my Uncle Ray's (the one he took to Spain, I believe), and I was to take great care of it and let him have it back in one piece.

I did have some concerns and worries regarding the trip, although I kept most of them to myself. This was the first time I was leaving my family and going away to stay with strangers for an entire week. How would I cope without Mom and the other kids? As much as the lack of space drove me crazy sometimes, they were as close to me as my own limbs somehow. And as rough as my upbringing was, the back yard was my home and where I felt safe. I was half-scared, half-excited, lying awake with such questions as 'What will the woman and the man be like?', 'Will they

like me?' And even 'What if they have a dog that bites me?'
– as though all country farms were overrun with rabid dogs
frothing at the mouth! Well, you never know... I think on
a subconscious level I may also have been wary of meeting
people from a different class, who might judge me for not
having the 'right' clothes or talking the right way.

Perhaps my parents had similar concerns. They looked
a little apprehensive as they stood on the street with a
small group of my siblings and friends congregating to
wave goodbye, as I embarked on my first ever trip away
on my own. Those were the days before it became fairly
commonplace for children to go away on school trips. As
Eileen's dad carried her pale and frail body to his car I
overheard my dad say to his mate that it was a rust bucket
and he wondered if we'd get there in one piece. But little
did we all know that within a week I'd return, almost a
transformed child – ruddier in the face, with a slightly
chubbier tummy, talking nineteen to the dozen about
the delights of Devon, to such an extent Mom probably
wished I'd never gone.

All my worries melted away almost as soon as I arrived
at the farm. The farmer's wife greeted us with a warm
smile and a chirpy-sounding 'Alright, my loves?' It was
the first time I'd heard such a different dialect and I had
a few difficulties understanding her to begin with. But I
remember thinking how warm and friendly the tone of
her voice was and she immediately put us at ease. I was
in disbelief as I took in the sights around us. It was like

something out of *Snow White* – the stone, cottage-styled bungalow, freshly mowed grass and birds tweeting as they landed on pink-blossomed trees. I had never seen anything like it before in my life.

All around us, fields and valleys stretched for miles, wrapped in a deep velvety green, such that I'd never seen before. I loved the strong aroma of the manure too – it smelt uplifting, healthy, fresh and inviting. Although the bungalow was small, with no more than two or three bedrooms, it seemed enormous to us.

Eileen smiled at the farmer's wife as she helped her dad carry her into the bedroom where we would stay. I was struck straight away by how clean and spotless it was. The sun was shining through the windows that were trimmed with lace curtains. There were two single-size beds with patchwork covers on them and plumped-up, pure cotton pillows edged with lace.

I looked around in amazement and said completely innocently: 'I wonder who else will share our beds?' The farmer's wife laughed so much that her tummy wobbled when she laughed, wiping away tears of mirth with her clean white apron. Her husband smiled and reassured us they were both for us. We looked at each other in amazement: we had this lovely room and bedroom all to ourselves.

I turned to them both and said: 'You're going to have a job on your hands getting us to leave this room, we'll never want to go home ever.'

Our cases were brought up and the farmer's wife quickly

unpacked them. It was as though we had our own valet – we were bewildered by this treatment. And rather than just the one chair to throw our clothes over, we had our own drawers and a beautiful wardrobe to hang them in. But one of the biggest luxuries for us both was to have our own beds, all to ourselves. They were singles but it was still wonderful to go to sleep each night without a smelly foot in my face or anticipating feeling the warmth of Alan's wee up my back – what bliss! On the first morning I woke to the waft of a beautifully cooked breakfast – sausages, fried eggs and the smell of freshly baked bread.

On the table sat a large pot of tea poured into delicate little china cups with red rose details around them and matching saucers – we each had our own tiny silver teaspoons and it tasted better than any tea we'd ever had before. The farmer's wife beamed and said, 'That will be the milk – straight from the cow.' My stomach was rumbling from the smells so I scoffed down two eggs, bacon, sausage, two doorstep pieces of fresh bread and butter, all swilled down with two cups of tea.

To our delight, the farmer's wife had also made some fruit scones. I managed to find room for them and we ate them with thick creamy butter – such a treat compared to the usual lard! Devonshire cream and homemade strawberry jam. Eileen and I looked at each other, our eyes widening as these unknown tastes melted in our mouths. I was surprised at how quickly we wolfed it all down and I wondered how we would cope with the rations once we returned home, though that was a long way off yet.

Rather than helping with clearing up or doing chores, the farmer's wife offered to show us round the yard to feed the chickens – they were a lot plumper than Mrs Griffin's chickens. There was quite a lot of mud and I was glad I'd brought my wellies. Some of the feed landed on them so I was swamped by about four chickens pecking at my feet. I didn't like the sensation at all and shooed them away. The farmer's wife laughed and said that they were just trying to get to know me. When we fed the chickens, I felt for Eileen though – she'd probably have loved nothing better than to stomp around in the mud, getting her feet dirty and pecked at.

Eileen and I helped out with the horses, brushing them and putting fresh hay down for them too. We also cleared up the horse muck that they used on the tomatoes and roses. Eileen was limited to what she could do in the wheelchair but enjoyed doing whatever she could manage.

The farmer's wife called us in to have milk and biscuits in the kitchen as an afternoon snack. Then we went for a walk to help Eileen's mobility but she seemed very weak and tired, so we put her back in the chair and I read a story to her before lunch. After a while we went back in the house – it was so warm in there with a roaring fire in the large living room. We sank back into comfy big chairs and just sat there, happy in the moment, reading to each other and chatting about our experiences of the day.

I helped fluff up Eileen's pillows. It seemed strange to have these seats all to ourselves and I think I asked a number of times if it was OK to sit in them. We were so relaxed that we began nodding off to sleep – I think it was the first time I'd ever had a siesta in my life! Eileen was soon snoring away in the big armchair. She'd just had a dose of her medication so I put it down to that. But the farmer's wife said it was the fresh country air – it tended to have that effect on most people when they weren't used to it.

We woke her when dinner – roast chicken – was served. Delicious as it was, I could hardly eat it after thinking of the chickens we'd played with earlier and wondered if it was one of the ones that had been pecking my feet! It was accompanied by fresh vegetables that had been grown on the farm and potatoes that tasted so fresh, followed by homemade apple pie and custard made with milk.

When we were in bed I felt so full and I thought of my family and wondered what they'd eaten that night. I felt a little homesick and sad, but that didn't stop me enjoying every single minute of having all that lovely space to myself. I was sleeping so soundly and peacefully each night, more than I ever had before in my life.

Throughout the week, the local doctor would check on Eileen's progress and administer more injections. A nurse also arrived each day to change her bandages. She removed the iron straps to massage ointment onto her thin legs and asked if I wanted to help – the nurse explained that it helped her circulation. We then helped her to walk with sticks.

Although we put her irons back on, she moved slowly and seemed a little stiff. On the first day she managed a few steps but definitely progressed throughout the week. She cried at times with the aches and pains but soon cheered up when she was given some fresh strawberries and cream and orange juice.

Each afternoon, I helped wash the dishes and tidy the bedrooms – the people there were so kind to us and I wanted to return the favours. The farmer's wife patted me on the head and said: 'You're a good girl, your friend is lucky to have you.' I replied: 'I'm the lucky one because I am well, and healthy, and living here on the farm is such a real treat.'

The biggest surprise was the bathroom. Never in our lives had we seen one this size. Back at our house there was just the tin bath on a rusty nail in the yard that was brought in front of the fire on Friday night. The lady that helped out with running the farmhouse was bathing Eileen and I went in to help. She was soaking in the tub with loads of bubbles that smelt so good. I washed her hair and plaited it for her and then had a soak in the tub myself, which was heaven. I felt guilty then because I felt I never wanted to go home to that hovel ever again. But all the while I remembered what Mom had warned me: I was not to forget my place because I was there as a companion for my friend – 'Only speak when you're spoken to and don't forget your manners – watch your Ps and Qs too!'

To me the kitchen seemed out of this world – I'd never

been somewhere the table was only for eating and we could take our time to enjoy the meal. It was as though I was seeing everything fresh and new for the first time, with a different pair of eyes – the carrots, fresh from the vegetable garden, still had green leaves on them, not like the ones we got from the Co-op, which always looked a bit sad and wilted by the time they reached our house. It was as though I'd stumbled across the Garden of Eden they talked about in Sunday School.

While our hostess chopped vegetables for dinner, she'd ask if we wanted any, which would never have happened back home – not because Mom was mean but because every pea or pod had to stretch to the seven of us. In this home, there were no jobs to do at meal times either. Normally I'd be shelling peas or peeling potatoes. Eileen and I would offer but she'd just shake her head and smile.

We couldn't believe that all the food laid upon the table was for us. The portions were at least three or four times bigger than what we were used to and we would go to bed each night with our bellies heaving. I wouldn't have known the difference between pork or beef but the meat tasted delicious with wholesome gravy, mashed potatoes and cabbage that hadn't been boiled within an inch of its life. I think it was the freshness that made it taste so good. Every main meal was followed by a pudding – normally an apple pie, made from apples from the orchard, all topped off with lashings of custard.

We'd never tasted food this good and often gobbled it

down without knowing what it was. We honestly thought we'd died and gone to heaven every night, not least when we were offered warm milk or hot chocolate. Even the biscuits were homemade – no broken packs from the Co-op here! Everywhere seemed bright and airy too. In comparison to the doom and gloom of the back-to-backs the light danced around the white painted walls.

We'd seen horses before on the streets dragging coal, but never ones as beautiful as their farmhorses. Whereas the ones down Arthur Street carrying coal looked scraggy and unkempt, these had gleaming chestnut manes, which the farmer let us brush – we had to stand up on a box to reach them. We were a bit daunted by the size of them – they seemed to tower over us. I was warned not to walk around the back of them, not that I would have done – I was far too cautious! Eileen couldn't walk or stand properly but she was able to sit on a horse properly and we each took turns trotting around the stables while they led us round. I was a little scared as I was so high up and wanted to get down as quickly as possible but Eileen loved it – it was the first time I'd seen her smile so widely. After being housebound, I think the new environment helped restore some faith and confidence in her ability to do physical activities. Although she wasn't able to walk, she enjoyed being pushed around the country lanes in her wheelchair – I think the fresh air was incredibly good for her and when she was too tired, we'd make daisy chains.

It breaks my heart when I think of it now – she never

once moaned or complained but occasionally let on how scared she was, never knowing if or when she was going to recover. I remember her saying how safe she felt on the farm too. Eileen had a very selfless and sweet attitude regarding her illness: she was always aware of the strain that it put on her parents. When she wasn't staying in the hospital for treatment her parents struggled to juggle their work and time to look after her. She really appreciated how much they looked after her when she was home and said how pleased she was that they'd get a rest while she was away. I knew how much her mom would be missing her though as she cried when she waved us goodbye.

We never saw much of the farmer, who was always up and gone in the mornings before we were awake. It was only at night when we all sat down to eat in the lovely farmhouse and then he would tell us about his day and ask us what we had done. But one morning we were woken up at half five to milk the cows – I didn't like the feel of it at all and didn't want to hurt the cow.

I was a bit scared of how big the cows were and the noises they made – I was scared they would whip me with their tail or squash me. I felt so small sitting next to them. But Eileen thought it was hilarious, as she sat in her wheelchair and had a go.

Every morning we would wake to the sound of birds chirruping away. We didn't even mind being woken by the cockerel at six each day – it never got on our nerves because it was a wonderful reminder that we were waking up in

Paradise. Eileen kept saying, 'Pinch me, I'm dreaming' whenever she woke up.

We never wanted our time there to end. I thought I'd miss my siblings but I really appreciated the peace and quiet, just the gentle background murmurings of new stimulating sounds that my ear gradually attuned to over the week – wood pigeons cooing, sheep bleating and clucking geese. Quite a contrast to what I was ordinarily used to – the cries of Barbara falling over in the yard or David getting his fingers stuck in the grate.

At the end of each day we were tired, but it was a happy exhaustion. We felt as though it was the right time to lay our heads upon the pillows too because we were completely in sync with nature and the cycles of the day. Preparing for bed was also a luxurious experience. When we first arrived it was a culture shock, not least to have someone make a fuss of us. Looking back, I realise the farmer's wife would have received money for hosting us, but nonetheless, she was incredibly kind and hospitable. Nothing was too much trouble and she treated us with untold respect and kindness. We felt it in the way she brushed our hair each night before bed or offered to help us in and out of the bath.

To bathe in warm water fresh from a tap all on my own without the usual two-in, two-out rigmarole was great. It was the first time I'd had a bath on my own as I'd not yet been to the baths down Green Lane so to have my own bath and bar of soap was a real novelty, as was the feel of the acrylic base rather than the tin beneath my feet. Plus, the bathroom had an indoor toilet – with its own working chain! The one in the yard at Arthur Street was always breaking.

I felt a little like the Princess from *The Princess and the Pea*. This was one of my favourite stories to read before bed at home, except I was experiencing the opposite of what she did – I was falling into the deepest sleeps every night and awaking refreshed and rested.

We never discussed the back-to-backs with the farmer's wife and for all we knew she may not even have known of their existence – there weren't any down South, they were much more prevalent in the industrial North. She was a very genuine and warm person and I never felt judged by her in the slightest, or her husband. However, I caught her looking at us a few times before dabbing her eyes with her apron as tears welled up in her eyes. I think she was especially moved when we were so grateful to her – we were constantly saying 'Is this for me? All of it?' and whenever she said 'Alright, my love? One egg or two?' we were baffled. A whole egg to ourselves? Whatever next!

I was so used to running around doing chores at home that it seemed strange to never be asked to do anything, not even tidy. It was so alien to have someone make a fuss of us. I loved my mom, and I still do, but this lady oozed a loveliness I've not forgotten – I just wanted to take her home.

That night I bathed and washed my hair because it was

the last night of our stay and I would miss this luxury. Eileen had to sit on the chair and I helped to wash her and do her hair. I brushed her fair hair till it shone like gold. The sun was bringing out a lovely glow to her cheeks and her freckles were appearing – I tried to count them each day to keep an eye on how many she was getting.

She could only get in the bath when the nurse or helper could take off her iron straps and was supervised at all times. She never moaned, and I helped to wash her down with a flannel and soap.

On our last day we picked wild flowers and gave them to the farmer's wife. She looked extremely touched as she dabbed at her eyes with her apron again. We were feeling sad as we got ready for bed knowing this was our last night in this lovely place – we both cried ourselves to sleep.

It was a week where it seemed the sun shone only for us. Both our spirits and health had been revived – not just from the fresh air and food but the kindness of strangers who seemed to genuinely care for us and ask for nothing in return. I think we both knew we'd never feel quite like this again. The next morning we woke to the sound of the cockerel for the last time and took one last look at the sweeping green fields out of our window. We tried to avoid each other's forlorn expressions.

I should have felt happy to return to the streets where I could play out till ten at night because I knew that poor Eileen didn't even have that option. After breakfast we kissed and hugged the farmer's wife. She hugged us and with tears in her eyes said what good girls we were and that she would miss us. We got in the car and waved until our hands nearly fell off. The farmer's wife had packed us a basket full of goodies for home – the sort of treats I knew would make my siblings' mouths water: scones and homemade jam in jars that weren't even recycled, not even a Robertson's jam sticker on them.

My brothers and sisters couldn't wait to get stuck in and listened in amazement when I told them about the orchard where the apple pie had come from. I didn't stop talking about it for weeks, despite Mom's stern warnings that I needed to come back down to earth because I was getting 'above my own station' and had been 'far too spoilt'. Behind these stock phrases though, I saw sadness in her eyes even then because I think she wished she were able to provide this for us.

I never saw the '*Darling Buds* Ma' ever again – I always wanted to save up some money in the Saturday Fund and return but it just never happened. Over the years I've thought about her a lot and wondered what happened to her. I've also tried to track down Eileen. Because she was ill she should have gone higher up the council's points system to be re-housed, but she was still in the back-to-backs when I left at eleven.

Sadly, it was all too easy to lose the close friendships forged once you left. I hope that Eileen did eventually recover from the wretched disease and that it didn't affect her long-term enjoyment of life. Sadly today, approximately 25 to 40 per cent of people who suffered from it as children are affected by post-polio syndrome (PPS). Symptoms normally appear 15–30 years after the initial illness and range from muscular weakness to pain and fatigue. Bless Eileen, I hope that she is well and happy wherever she is, and I thank her for the best holiday of my life – nothing as yet has even come close.

16

Christmas and Sixpence Scams

Is bleak as our winters were, Christmas gave us moments of colour, light and glimmers of hope, never failing to lift our spirits each year. Mom and Dad didn't have a lot but they would really push the boat out for us to make it a time filled with cheer. For a week or two, our home was filled with the warm and uplifting scents of chicken, turkey, apples, oranges and nuts roasting on the fire. Even the fire seemed to crackle and pop with a newfound cheer – and we all knew how much Mom had scrimped and saved for this. She always knew how to haggle with the barrow boys in the market and would get the best vegetables, from carrots to parsnips and sprouts. One of her favourite expressions was 'Don't be skinny', which meant 'Don't scrimp' – she'd always persuade them to stick another potato or two in.

I think all of us developed a good head for business from her. At this time of year we'd often hang around the market until the end of the day when many of the vegetables ended up on the floor anyway – we'd scramble for them in the Christmas rush.

As with any other time of year we stretched our resources, including every last piece of cardboard or paper we could find – I loved making paper chains of all different colours and we'd hang these around the house, from any hook or nail we could, in between the drying of Terry nappies! We also loved to make decorations at school, which all helped Mom in hindsight. And Christmas wouldn't be Christmas without the fresh sprig of holly and a small real fir tree from the market, brought in on Christmas Eve, which we decorated with a fairy and tinsel bought from Woolworths.

One year, Dennis took it upon himself to let us in on a shocking secret – that Father Christmas was no more magical or faraway than our very own father! And he could prove it. Ever the wily one, he carefully placed a pile of books at the top of our open attic door before we fell asleep on Christmas Eve. But we didn't want Dennis to be right and hoped Father Christmas would come as promised to prove him wrong. We nodded off to sleep and awoke not to the sound of festive sleigh bells but Dad effin' and blindin' as a pile of books came crashing down to the floor, narrowly missing his head. It must have confused the hell out of him, especially if he'd had a few in the pub. He shouted out: 'Right, you lot! If you don't believe, I'll give these toys to children that do!' We cried ourselves to sleep that night but still woke to find presents at the foot of our bed. Maybe Father Christmas had a word with Dad to soften him up.

One of the first treats on Christmas morning was porridge made with water and a drop of milk with a small spoonful of sugar. We were still on rations until the early fifties, although the shops seemed to be packed with goodies. We'd press our noses up against the windows of the shops down 'The Cov' marvelling at all the toys, chocolate boxes, cakes and fruit – sometimes they'd get stuck to the pane because it was so freezing.

We were still only allowed two ounces of most produce. On this day though, we ate like kings and queens and went to bed with full bellies. After porridge, we put on our best and most warm clothes and ploughed our way through the snow to St Aidan's Church on a handmade go-kart for the afternoon service. Yes, I'm not just looking back with rose-tinted specs on – it would snow every Christmas without fail. The winters were freezing back then, they're far milder now.

David would steer the way on the go-kart while Dennis clutched the sixpence Dad had entrusted us with, in his new gloves that Auntie Lil had knitted – we never tired of balaclavas and gloves each year because we were always losing them. This is when I envied Dennis his *Daily Mail* boots as the studs gave him proper grip. I had wellies on but my feet were frozen in them.

The sixpence was for the collection plate. But Dennis had a new money-making scam in place. He placed the sixpence down, looked straight into the eyes of the woman taking the plate around, who was smiling down at him kindly, and took three pence back. Six pence did seem rather a lot to part with, especially at Christmas.

I'll never forget the look on that woman's face – she went as red as a tomato while Dennis looked away and carried on singing angelically to 'O Little Town of Bethlehem', as though butter wouldn't melt in his mouth. David and I did our utmost not to burst out laughing for the rest of the service – we could barely contain ourselves throughout the solemn sermon. When we finally got out the three of us fell about laughing in the snow outside, struggling to maintain our balance on the slippery ice. Every time I thought of her startled expression I would collapse into fits of giggles again. We were overjoyed when Dennis said, 'OK, what will it be then? Sherbet, arrowroot or liquorice?'

My mouth started watering at the prospect – well, it was Christmas after all. We convinced ourselves that God would understand as we slid off to the tiny sweet shop on the corner of Arthur Street and Herbert Road to stock up on kali, rainbow drops and aniseed balls. However, sweets aren't just for Christmas – Sundays became extra special as we looked forward to our weekly treat. I just had to make sure I looked away each time David retrieved the three pence. As time went on, he became even more nonchalant about it.

We wiped away the sugary evidence from our mouths with our coat sleeves as we trooped back into the warmth of the fire and our small living room, where the table was set. It smelt amazing but I felt a little sick from the sugar hit. Mom's gravy was always particularly hearty and thick – she'd add the juice from the meat with a pinch of salt and pepper. I loved it spread all over the roast potatoes crisped up on the fire. We were never short of sausages as she worked in the factory and was given a bonus amount at Christmas. Dad would carve the turkey and Mom would dress up the table for Christmas with a coloured sheet red chenille tablecloth. Christmas pudding always went in the brewus boiler, wrapped in a muslin cloth along with everyone else's. Then we'd cover it in swathes of custard – a ultra-special treat from the Co-op. We'd all be stuffed full at this point but still found room for chocolates and nuts – it was Dad's job to crack the nuts.

Dennis and David would go to borrow extra chairs from Nancy Nee – we were short of space as it was, but were always joined by Auntie Lil and Ray. Christmas wouldn't have been the same without them or the family games we played after. My favourite was 'Spin the Bottle' – if it pointed at you, you had to sing, dance or tell a joke. This came naturally to some of us more than others. Dennis would grab any opportunity to tell a joke, although we'd laugh hysterically when he'd start off with 'There was an Englishman, an Irishman and a Scotsman…' then tail off as he forgot the punchline. Dad always chose to sing – he had a good voice, even after a bottle of port or sherry he'd got on the strap from Mrs Beighton, so we didn't mind too much. His speciality number was Bing Crosby's 'True Love' – he wouldn't go so far as to put his sailor suit on (which is what Bing wore in the film *High Society*) before he belted it out, but his accordion might make an appearance if he was drunk enough.

He would look into Mom's eyes and croon away. Occasionally, she would join in on the Grace Kelly parts if the sherry gave her a bit of Dutch courage but it was Dad's turn to shine really. He loved this song and used to sing it down the Birmingham Social Club on a Sunday. I still remember all the lyrics. Auntie Lil enjoyed singing too, especially Irish numbers. I often wondered if she'd had an Irish romance at some point – whenever she sang 'When Irish eyes are smiling, sure they'll steal your heart away' her own eyes would mist over a little. Uncle Ray would always bring a bit of culture with him too. He went to Spain every summer so would bring back something typically Spanish – a tea towel with flamenco dancers on it or a doll for Mom to put on the sideboard along with all the others he brought back every year.

Looking back, I don't know how we all squeezed around the table but it didn't matter, there was somehow enough room, food and hospitality for everyone. Mom always said that if you give with a good heart the food multiplies, and sure enough, it seemed to. There was always plenty of turkey left over for sandwiches later in the evening and she would make a gorgeous soup from the leftover bones for Boxing Day. Later, the Nees family came over, along with the Jeys. Carols were sung and as long as Dad kept quiet about what he thought of Mickey, no stools were broken – just the odd jam jar or glass.

We didn't have a spare room of course but Auntie Lil and Ray would stay the night, which was a real treat – we'd push the two armchairs together for Ray while Lil had the sofa. Luckily, Boxing Day didn't bring any Uncle Ernie punch-ups either: we would wake to yet more blissful aromas of bacon and eggs, an extremely rare treat. Us kids would be allowed a dip in the fat, half a fried egg and the rind off the bacon – adults and guests were served the best first. There were always pots of tea to swill it down, with half a teaspoon of sugar as a Christmas treat.

Despite the colder temperatures, there was still no escaping the quick swill – faces and hands had to be clean whatever the weather. We'd put on our new Auntie Lil knitwear and play in the street with all the other children on Arthur Street. We always wanted to have the biggest of everything – we had a reputation to live up to – and our snowmen were no exception. It was completely silent on the streets but for the odd squawk of a child getting smacked in the face by one of Dennis's extra-large snowballs – no coalman trawling down the street with his horse and cart for my brothers to run after and jump on the back of.

17

The Bull Ring Market, Barrow Boys and the City of a Thousand Trades

In 1729, when topographers Samuel and Nathaniel Buck came to paint Birmingham, they placed their easel on a spot in the south-west of the town, looking north. They looked down upon a simple skyline of rolling hills and rows of rather pleasant town houses, not yet blocked by hundreds of factories billowing out fumes across the city. From the picture they eventually painted, it looks rural and peaceful.

The skyline was to change dramatically, though. By 1750, the city's population had grown from 11,400 to 23,688. As with many cities, Birmingham's physical location contributed to this – early on, entrepreneurs were keen to profit from its close proximity to the coal and iron deposits of South Staffordshire. Although no thick fog clouds the landscape today, the lower town still has a reputation for a metalworking tradition that stretches back at least 800 years. But it was home to thousands of other trades too. Many of the city's population, including those who lived in the back-to-backs down Hurst Street, were employed in bone making – used to make toothbrushes, knife handles and spoons.

What I find fascinating though is that button making was the city's greatest industry throughout the eighteenth and early nineteenth centuries. By 1851, 5,000 people were employed as button makers. It makes me chuckle, not least because I wonder if that's why dear Auntie Lil collected so many over the years. When she died, all I wanted for an heirloom was her red OXO tins that overflowed with beautiful buttons of all different colours, shapes and sizes.

Lil never wasted anything – she cut off all buttons and zips before giving clothes to the rag man, saving them for years. Although she had so many, she knew just the button to use that would spice up any ordinary dress or cardigan from the market.

She also sewed buttons on to pieces of card to sell for extra money. I think she would have loved nothing more than to work somewhere like Taylor's button works in the 1740s, working on the hand-operated machines, stamping, pressing and attaching the shank (for some buttons, a small metal piece that provides space between the button and the garment).

My friend June, who lived next door to Auntie Lil,

and I loved playing with these buttons for hours, making up all sorts of different uses for them. To us they were never just buttons and became anything we wanted them to be – rings, money, jewellery, sweets or biscuits. My upbringing was tough but children have an innate instinct to play and there were no limits to our imagination. We could make something from literally nothing – and it never cost a penny.

Beneath St Martin's Church lies the Bull Ring, where the market has thrived since 1154, ever since Peter de Bermingham, a local landowner, was granted a charter of marketing rights from King Henry II. Initially, the site was used for textiles but over the centuries it gained a reputation for its flourishing grocery and meat trades, one that remains today.

And for families like ours who were struggling, the Bull Ring and its markets provided a crucial supply of goods. The Rag Market operated on Tuesday and Saturday afternoons and sold the sort of items you would find in second-hand shops today – clothes, furniture, knick-knacks, and even damaged crockery. Next to the Market Hall was Woolworths, which helped serve people on far lower incomes too – not many items cost more than sixpence.

Going to the market was always exciting for me – from a small age I remember being thrilled by its vibrant atmosphere. The smells hit me as soon as I walked in – the earthy gritty dirt from the potatoes and vegetables fresh from the countryside. All around me I could hear the sounds of the barrow boys competing with their rivals, desperate to shout out an even better deal at the tops of their lungs – 'Buy your bananas, apples, oranges, the best in town!'. Us Brummies were used to haggling our way through life and there was probably no finer example of this in action than down the market, as people shoved and pushed to get the best deal, knowing their next meal depended on it. But amidst the jostling there was laughter, joy and jokes, and a sense of seizing the opportunity of the moment. The lively and bustling atmosphere hasn't changed today, just the variety of cuisine now available – from Polish to Bengali and Somali.

After he left school at fifteen, Ray, my husband, started helping out his older brothers Harry and Roy, who worked at J.V. White, one of the largest fruit merchants at the time, right opposite Smithfield Market. This was a great help for their mother because it meant they never went without food. Roy worked as a groundsman and was up early at five in the morning when the market was already rammed with vans and barrow boys searching for the best deals. Brooks Vaults and other pubs in the area were some of the few places at this time where you could buy alcoholic beverages in the early morning. They had a special licence so that they could cater for all the traders. (A groundsman offloaded different types of produce – apples, oranges, potatoes, and so on – in their bags or sacks, which would be neatly stacked and samples opened for customers to see and handle. When a deal was done by the salesman he gave a groundsman the list of produce the customer had bought. The groundsman would ask the buyer where his vehicle was parked, then put the order on the wheelbarrow, and take it and load it all on to the vehicle; sometimes he would have to make numerous trips if it was a big order. The customer would give the groundsman a tip for doing this, some more than others. The really big customers sent lorries inside the market to be loaded – until fork-lift trucks were introduced to market life everything was loaded and unloaded by hand.)

Ray started on £1, 2 shillings and 6 old pennies a week (£1.125, equivalent to about £25 today) – not a king's ransom but with tips and all the fruit and vegetables he could have for nothing, it was better than a lot of other menial jobs. He also credits it as a wonderful learning curve into working life, where he met honest, humorous, tolerant, decent people, who would help anyone if they could. In particular, he remembers two salesmen that Roy worked with: George Dudley and Johnnie Vick, well known and much-loved for the cheeky repartee they had with each other.

The market would normally go quiet around 10.30. They'd told Roy to start tidying up the pitch, to move and re-stack the unsold produce. On this particular pitch it was mainly apples. George and Johnnie were doing the books when a regular customer offered them two 'nice pieces of pork pie' he had left over – a large and small piece. He offered first to Johnnie, who quick as a flash took the large piece. George objected to this and said it was 'disgusting' that he'd taken the large slice and left the small for him. 'If you were a gentleman, you would have taken the small piece and left the large one for me,' he noted. At this, Johnnie said to George: 'If you had been offered first, which piece would you have taken?' George replied: 'The small one, of course.' John said: 'Well, in that case, I don't know what you're moaning at because you've got the small piece!' He burst out laughing and walked off out the market.

After the *Windrush* had brought in the first wave of Caribbean and West Indian immigrants in 1948, we began to see more exotic, brightly coloured vegetables of all shapes, colours and sizes, such as plantains, okra and mango – bear in mind that a banana was still pretty exotic to us back then!

Ray's other brother, Harry, worked for J.V. White for a number of years and was one of their top salesmen. The pitch he worked on sold mainly to black immigrants who had businesses in and around Birmingham – he sold sweet potatoes, mangoes and a lot of West Indian produce. He had a great relationship with his customers, even though at that time black immigrants had to pay cash for everything they bought because they weren't allowed credit, nor could they pay by cheque. But they loved Harry and trusted him, and as a mark of respect, they nicknamed him 'Black 'arry' and he was soon known by that name all round the market.

Later, he set up his own business selling all the same exotic fruits, which he made a great success of for many years. He made many West Indian friends and enjoyed many visits to their families in the countries they'd emigrated from.

The barrow boys were part of a long and rich tradition that started back in the nineteenth century – from the early mornings they haggled for the best fruit and vegetable deals they could get from some of the biggest dealers down Jamaica Row, such as Walter Glover and J.V. White, who no longer exist today. There, they loaded large iron barrows with fruit and vegetables, which doubled up as a stall once they settled down in the outdoor retail market in the Bull Ring. The name of the wholesaler they'd bought from would often be painted in white on the side of the barrow.

Most of the barrow boys were generous, good souls. While we sat in the gutter taking in the hustle and bustle, our eyes would grow wider at the sheer quantities of food that were wheeled around in front of us – so near, yet so far! I think some of the lads could see we were hungry – they'd take pity on us and give away the bruised apples at the end of the day to us. They'd hand out samples too – slicing up nuts and oranges for us to try. In between helping undernourished kids and shouting to everyone about how lovely their bananas were, they'd tell any pretty-faced girl going by how lovely her smile was. The noise could be deafening but we loved it.

One figure who's never left my mind is the lady who

used to stand in the market selling brown paper bags. I can still hear her voice ringing out across the din of the market as clearly today as the bells of St Martin's when I shop in the market – 'Get your carrier – 'andy carrier bag!' This phrase has become as much a part of Brummie jargon as 'I'm goin' all around the Wrekin' or 'You're half-soaked, you are!' ('I'm taking the long way round', especially if someone is being long-winded or off the point – the Wrekin being a hill in Shropshire – and 'You're a bit dim,' respectively).

She probably wasn't as old as she appeared to us but she reminded me a bit of the tuppence lady from *Mary Poppins* – wrapped up in all weathers with her black shawl and boots to keep warm. She was toothless with squinting, small beady eyes, and grey hair as wispy and fragile as her fingerless-gloved hands that clutched her carrier bags.

We bought them at only a copper or two ('couple or three' in Brummie speak) because she was so sweet and friendly to us kids – always telling us to wrap up warm on cold days. I never saw her miss a day's work. She always had a cup of tea in her hand – a polystyrene cup that someone had bought for her from the market cafe. She's so deeply ingrained in Brummie mythology that her true identity is still discussed on forums today. Sometimes, I still listen for her voice in the market, and I've often wondered what happened to her.

The Kings Hall Market opened in 1897 as The New Central Hall at the lower end of Corporation Street. In

1932 it was converted to an indoor market and over the years parts of it were used for various things such as an amusement arcade. I can still remember the smell of fresh fish as I walked in, where eels, crabs and snails still wriggled in big containers. The sight of rabbits dangling from hooks made my tummy rumble and my mouth water. It closed in the early sixties and after a fire in 1963 was demolished shortly after.

In 1964, the Birmingham Bull Ring Centre was opened by the Duke of Edinburgh, Prince Philip, alongside Herbert Manzoni. The first indoor city-centre shopping centre in the UK, it had cost an estimated £8 million and was inspired by American malls. It was designed to herald a grand new era of cosmopolitan shopping but was not the success they were expecting. In my opinion, it's the markets that remain the true social heartland of the city.

Birmingham's reputation as 'the city of a thousand trades' had long been established by the end of World War II, but its international reputation as the workshop of the world attracted many migrant workers too. Just as folk travelled from the country to the city during the Industrial Revolution for the promise of all the riches Birmingham offered, hundreds of people from Britain's former West Indian colonies travelled even further across the Atlantic for similar riches. But not only were they looking for work and a better life, they were also looking for a place called home in their 'mother country'.

It wasn't to be as straightforward as all that for them

though, unfortunately. Many immigrants found out only too quickly that although their labour was wanted – to fill a glut of unskilled jobs within industry – there was no accompanying warm welcome. As the *Birmingham Mail* reported, many who arrived in the city decided within as little as three hours it was the most inhospitable place they'd ever visited. Not surprising with the 'No blacks, no dogs, no Irish' signs awaiting them in the housing market. It seems the Brummie hospitality I know and love so well sadly had certain conditions that came with it back then. Of course, that is not to say that this sentiment was ingrained in every Brummie but I did witness hostility towards immigrants in my neighbourhood, not least from my own dad.

Despite the fact he'd been in the Navy and was a well-travelled man who spoke highly of the beauty of the many lands he'd visited – from Japan to China – he nursed a high suspicion of all foreigners. As well as Caribbean and West Indian immigrants, there were many Czech and Polish exiles that ended up in the West Midlands for various reasons. Some were associated with the Air Force. For almost three years – between 1940 and 1943 – the Polish 308 Squadron was based at Baginton Airfield in Warwickshire, flying Hurricanes and Spitfires to help defend the Midlands.

Many Polish servicemen remained in the Midlands, often finding homes across the region. And some ended up in Small Heath. I often think now it would have been interesting to hear their stories, but Dad specifically instructed us never to speak to them. Again, we didn't ask why at the time. 'Why' just wasn't a word that tended to come out of our mouths and we trusted his opinion. Looking back, I'm surprised, especially as many of them were our allies, or refugees who had fled a common enemy, so in hindsight it makes little sense. It's something I would ask him now if he was alive. Some of it perhaps stemmed from personal vendettas; he wasn't too fond of the Irish either and I suspect this was from something as daft as a punch-up in the pub with one once.

Our own demographic on Arthur Street was also altered when a substantial group of black families moved into the corner of the street, just past the Prince Arthur pub. It was a particularly large house that I think must have been a shop from years ago from the size of the windows in the front, so it looked massive to us. Although considerably bigger than what we were used to, there was clearly not enough space for them as many arrived with their extended families. It looked cramped and uncomfortable and no doubt they were dealing with many of the same squalid housing conditions that we were, not to mention the fact they were also often turned away from lots of accommodation.

I was curious about them and their stories as I walked past but never made an attempt to communicate, as per Dad's instructions. We would just occasionally stare blankly at each other, no smiles or waves. I'm very pleased to say that attitudes have altered a lot over the past seventy years and I'm proud to live in such a vibrant and thriving multi-cultural city.

18

Mom's Stockings Save the Day on Our Family Holiday to Weston-super-Mare

'The smile in smiling Somerset' was the slogan emblazoned across Weston-super-Mare tourist posters back in the fifties. Having visited many different glorious holiday destinations over the years, I realise that Weston-super-Mare with its low tides – suitably named Weston-super-Mud – sorry-looking pier and equally sorry-looking donkeys isn't the most glamorous of seaside haunts. But for us, a trip to the coast may as well have been a trip to Hawaii, especially as Birmingham is the furthest city from the sea. Before 'staycations' became a trendy term, trips to the coast were increasingly common throughout the fifties, even for the poorest of families, especially as road networks across the country improved.

One summer holiday we were outside playing when

we heard an almighty bang – we turned around to see an old van with dirty brown windows at the side making its way down the street. Dad had saved up hard to buy it – the woodwork and chenille rug orders were continuing to bring in helpful extra income. The thought of getting in your own machine to go somewhere else still seemed almost sci-fi to us – yes, we'd been on buses, but the thought that you could be in control of your own destiny whenever you wanted was amazing to us.

This van was a portal to distant lands across the UK, linked together by motorways and A-roads – dotted with flashy new diners, for the first motorway service stations were inspired by US-style restaurants. Not surprisingly though, our first outing to this brave new world wasn't to be quite as straightforward as we thought, not least with the set of wheels we had to get us there. The seven of us were crammed in the back, along with our holiday essentials – namely an old scouts' tent Dad had bought from the church jumble sale. He'd also bought a Primus stove, sleeping bags and a groundsheet from the Army & Navy stores. Mom took some extra blankets to keep us warm too.

We didn't have much chance to take in the glories of the English countryside whizzing past our windows. Every five minutes we would chirp up with a chorus of 'Are we nearly there yet?' much to the annoyance of our parents. In those days, there were no iPads to divert our attention and with seven of us squished in the back we were soon boiling, even with the windows wound down. I think I held Philip or Stephen most of the way – this was before safety belts, of course. This was also in the days before most exhaust pipes were fitted with filters so we were breathing in some fairly noxious fumes the whole way. It wasn't long before we began to feel incredibly tired and sick and our excitement started to wane.

Just as we were beginning to think things couldn't get any worse, we heard a rumbling noise and noticed smoke coming from the bonnet of the van. We looked on in horror as we felt the van shudder and then heard an almighty bang. We all screamed out loud – even Dad!

Ever the trained military man, Dad immediately instructed us not to panic. And we needn't have. As always, he had the answers to our problems – his ability to recycle whatever was within reach seemed to be hardwired into his DNA. On this particular journey, it was Mom's stockings that saved us. She wasn't too happy to sacrifice them but there was little time to get precious so she whipped them off without protest – being left stranded on the road to Weston-super-Mare was not a great alternative anyway. Within ten minutes Dad had transformed them into a makeshift fan belt and topped up the radiator with the tap water Mom had given us in a bottle for the journey. He poked around in the bonnet for a bit, then off we went. It wasn't to be plain sailing from there on, though – Mom had a map to direct him but obviously had had little experience of navigating the roads, so Dad ended up taking a wrong turn. Eight hours later, we entered the campsite at Weston-super-Mare.

Although it was a tough trip, our spirits were lifted to catch our first-ever sight of the sea – we'd been looking out for a glimpse of it ever since we'd set off. Even though it was starting to get dark by that point, we could see it twinkling beyond the horizon as we rounded the corner. We all headed to the window, pushing each other out of the way, much to the annoyance of our parents who were trying to concentrate on driving. Every time we took this journey, we would argue over who had actually seen it first. Most of the time it was Dennis, of course. As the eldest it was almost his birthright, but we didn't really care in the end – it was as though we were seeing it for the first time every time anyway. It was absolutely wonderful, like something you only dream about. We'd seen the sea at the pictures but to see it in reality took our breath away, not least for what it signified for us – freedom, space, fresh air. We made several trips there in the summer and the journeys were rarely any less eventful. The van broke down almost every trip if the radiator overheated or ran dry, but Dad had an ingenious solution to this too – turns out our wee from various rest stops along the way doubled as a fantastic tank lubricant!

As soon as we found the campsite my dad, along with Dennis, David and Alan, put the tent up. It was dark by then but yet again, Dad's military training saved the day as they erected it in no time, with him calling out instructions to them. The tent alone looked bigger than the whole of our tiny back-to-back house – I'd never seen anything so enormous and the campsite we were on seemed to stretch for miles too.

Mom and I got the old Primus paraffin stove going that Dad had bought from the Army & Navy Stores and set about cooking eggs, sausages and making a brew that we'd been dying for throughout the journey. She'd already packed up enough food to last a few days – corned beef with brown sauce was one of our staple and favourite snacks. One of the main highlights of this first holiday away was experiencing the joy of collecting fresh milk and freshly laid eggs from the farmer down the road, who also owned the campsite.

We were all extremely tired so we washed our faces and hands – a quick swill as usual under the outdoor pump in the centre of the campsite. But we were excited to see there was a shower block with running warm water, a luxury we indulged in for the next week.

Our first night in the tent felt very exciting too. For once I felt like a member of the Famous Five – I'd always fantasised about lying out on beds made of fern or bracken, and now here I was, almost sleeping out under the stars! The tent probably only measured around four metres by four, but it was a joy not to have Dennis's foot in my face or Alan pressed up against my back. But this blissful state as we settled down onto the groundsheet with our blankets wasn't to last for long. I was just dropping off when we started to hear the first spots of rain on the tent. It was quite a peaceful sound at first – I liked hearing it tap gently against the canvas – but as the full wrath of 'Bill's mother' unleashed itself, we were to have our first experience sampling the delights of a typical British summer holiday.

We were used to water coming in through a hole in the roof in the attic of the back-back-back, but we hadn't brought a bucket with us. Soon, the rain was soaking through to our blankets that we had taken off our beds at home. Dad scurried about looking for a torch but decided it was too dark to try and repair it. He told the boys to move into the area where it wasn't so damp while me, Mom, Barbara and Philip, who was little more than a year at the time, went to sleep in the van. Mom bundled up Philip – whimpering a little at being disturbed – into a blanket.

It was dry in there, but I couldn't sleep – the rain was making such a noise on the roof of the van. And I was also worried that we would have to go home if Dad couldn't fix the tent and I really wanted to go to the beach! Eventually I fell asleep to the sound of a sheep bleating in the distance, who sounded equally fed up to be caught out by the weather.

Next morning we woke to sunshine streaming in through the van and the sound of the boys laughing and chasing each other in the fields. It was lovely to see the camp in all this light, the gloom of the previous evening melted away into the velvety green that surrounded us. Dad had almost fixed the tent and Mom fried up more eggs on the one pan we'd brought and boiled up some water for tea. After breakfast we all set off for the beach.

Well, it took us half an hour to walk to the beach and the tide was out – Weston-super-Mud was living up to its name! But the sun was shining and people were smiling. Every time we took a step towards the sea it seemed to tease us by moving further away as the sun twinkled on the horizon line that you could never quite reach. The sand felt slushy and cold beneath our feet, but it wouldn't prepare us for the chill of the sea – so much colder than any pool I'd dipped my toe in. It was worth the wait, though. I squealed as Dennis ran on ahead and turned to splash me. It was as though a rush of ice had stabbed my belly, but it forced me to wade in deeper. Often, Barbara and I would just paddle unless it was warm enough to swim, but the boys were determined to look as tough as possible, even on the colder, cloudier days. They loved to show off and prove they could bear the freezing temperatures. We were used to the cold from the back-to-backs but they would risk hypothermia to show how tough they were – they looked absolutely frozen as they emerged from the waters covered in seaweed, crabs hanging from their hair. We'd laugh hysterically at the state of them, while they just looked incredibly pleased with themselves.

Mom made egg and bacon sandwiches or jam on bread

as an extra-special holiday treat. Sometimes there was even a cake that she'd made before we went away. They were lapped up greedily after we'd been playing cricket on the beach with a bat and wicket that Dad had made. We played with other kids who said we 'sounded funny' – I've got used to this over the years as I've visited other places, but they sounded odd to us too, with their West Country burr.

We built sandcastles and Barbara and I had the important job of judging whose was best. At times like this it was hard not to fall out, but never for too long. We'd round off the day with a game of tig (the local word for tag) and sing songs on the beach.

I remember being genuinely exhausted by the end of the day, after we'd eaten beans on toast or fried egg on dip in fat (bread dipped into the fat in which the bacon and eggs had been cooked), all swilled down with a lovely hot cup of tea around the campfire (or our Primus stove at least!). We'd crawl into bed, worn out but happy to be alive. We never had much money to spare on these trips away and I don't remember us having any typical holiday treats such as ice cream or fish and chips but it didn't matter. It's something of a cliché but the best things in life really are free. You couldn't beat the fun and freedom found running around in the fresh air, with the waves crashing in the background. Or the genuine smile on Mom's face as she saw us frolicking about in this open space with no brick walls or brewus separating us from nature. We might have had cardboard in our shoes but all the class structures in the world couldn't come between us and this wide space we had to run around in. Dead-end kids or not, the feel of the sand between our toes and the wind in our hair came for free.

I never wanted the holiday to end – I didn't want to return to the feeling of being cramped, four of us in a bed, ever again. When we arrived home our house seemed even smaller than before. As we wearily unpacked our things and climbed back into our tiny bed, I vowed I would have a house in the country and a bed all to myself one day.

1

Touting for Business at The Blues, Getting Caught Scrumping and Teenage Heartthrob Tommy Steele

We had the run of our street back in the fifties. With so few cars on the streets they were ours to play whatever games we wanted – everything from Skip Rope to Kiss Chase. This became a particular favourite when I developed a crush on Jack Oliver, who lived up the street and was in my year at school. He had lovely dark curly hair and a wicked smile – all the girls liked him and I would feel quite jealous if he kissed anyone else. It was none other than an innocent peck on the cheek but my first foray into navigating the complexities of romantic relationships, while a lot more fun and less complicated! This first flutter with romance was not to be and I soon learned you can't hurry or chase love! We still remembered each other years later when we caught each other's glance in a pub – no chasing around the chairs or tables this time, though, and he'd lost some of that lovely curly black hair. But we had a chat about the old days and discussed how unrecognisable Arthur Street was, with all the houses demolished. There were no neighbours there now, telling kids to 'Clear off' or 'Get up your own end and play'. And long gone are the days when you saw children playing in the street.

I can barely differentiate between the rules of football and rugby and it's only recently that I found out that ELO's 'Mr Blue Sky' is the Birmingham Blues' anthem (although its official anthem is Sir Harry Lauder's 1924 hit 'Keep Right On to the End of the Road', after the club's legendary Scottish winger of the mid-1950s, Alex Govan, was heard singing it; it is still often sung before, during and after matches today, and is known to fans as 'KRO'). Despite my general indifference to the game though, I couldn't help but get caught up in the excitement the team brought to our streets when they played at their grounds at St Andrew's, all but an eight-minute walk away from us in Arthur Street.

The boys loved playing football on the street but those streets were off-limits on a Saturday when a match was on, chock-a-block full of beautiful cars. Even back then, football was still quite an expensive spectator sport – the minimum admission price was 1s 9d in 1950 (not quite 9p, but equivalent to about £2 now), so it was out of our price range, for sure. But we felt a sense of pride knowing The Blues were playing, not least for the fact it attracted some well-off punters to our streets. Well, certainly better off than us – they had cars for a start. Only around 6 per cent of the population had cars in 1955 so they were an impressive sight. Our eyes boggled at the row of shiny metal that snaked its way round our streets – from Morris Minors (the first British car to sell a million) to Rovers, with their wooden and leather interiors.

Ever the entrepreneur, Dennis, yet again, spotted some money making potential. As soon as a car pulled up, he'd be there in a flash with a ready and willing smile – 'I'll mind your car for you, mister!' – before they trotted off to the match. It was never just the one we minded, of course – Dennis and David were like businessmen proud of the number of cars they'd been left in charge of – 'I've got six cars!' they'd boast. When the other kids started to get in on the act, Dennis began marking out territory – he'd place wooden boxes (as though they were traffic cones) to save the parking space for drivers and would encourage them to move, even if they'd already parked, into 'his land' – normally the space outside the Jeys' house. Come rain or snow, we'd find them a place.

I never knew one car from another – I could just about remember the colour – but the boys were sharp as ninepence and knew every model and exactly what car belonged to whom. Professional as ever, Dennis sometimes wrote the registration numbers down, along with their descriptions and whether they were a Blues fan or an away team supporter.

Sometimes David or Alan would get a bucket and wipe the windows down to make sure they looked busy just before the drivers returned. Most of the time they'd leave us girls who were playing Hopscotch to mind them, while they climbed over the fence at half-time to watch the rest of the match. Then they'd race back before the end and wait for the drivers to collect their cars. It got confusing at times – you'd have to remember every fan by the number on the back of his football shirt and you had to be alert and quick off the mark to outwit the other kids – often there were fights over who was looking after whose cars.

You could make up to five bob (25p, equivalent to about £4.50 today) looking after someone's car. It was another way to pool some extra money together for Mom – if we didn't do a detour to the sweetshop, of course. The drivers in turn were happy to pay up because their precious cars were safe without a scratch on them. They paid whatever they wanted but some were more grateful and generous than others. People would obviously pay a lot more if their team had won too. All in all, we could make about two pounds or more between us on a good day. We put money in our savings tin for trips to the Kingston Picture House, sweets and chips. Needless to say, Saturday afternoons were pretty busy up 'our end'.

Sometimes I joined Dennis, David and Alan on their scrumping adventures. They'd normally pick the posher houses down Coventry Road – to us they seemed like kings, with their semi-detached homes and fruit trees in their very own gardens. I used to keep an eye out for the local bobby while the boys climbed up walls and clambered over fences to pinch apples. I'd lift my dress to catch whatever they threw down so they wouldn't bruise. We were nimble and quick as anything, but one day we got caught red-handed by a couple of policemen. As they marched us back up our end I had loads of apples cupped in my dress. I was so embarrassed – people were looking at us as though we were criminals – while the boys were just annoyed we'd been caught.

I think the police were actually quite subdued when they made it to our place – maybe it was a shock for them to venture into the slums and see how the other half lived. Perhaps pinching a few apples made a lot more sense when they realised how poverty-stricken we were. They mumbled something along the lines of: 'There'll be serious consequences if it happens again' and slipped away. Of course, we never did stop and our parents never got too cross with us about it either – Mom made the most delicious apple pies so it was worth the risk!

Most of the time I got on with my brothers. They were kind and tolerated my more 'girly' preferences. Sometimes they could be right little terrors to my toys, though – my favourite doll – Susan – endured frequent trips to the dolls' hospital because they used to poke her eyes out and crack her face. I sometimes had to wait weeks for her to be returned as we had to save up the money to pay for her to be fixed. But Auntie Lil used to say it was because there were lots of other sick dollies that needed help.

I couldn't afford comics but used to cut out dolls with

my friends, Valerie and Ann. We'd make them out of thin cardboard and colour them in to create our own style of dresses – anything from school uniform to fancy party dresses. They were often the kind of dresses I dreamt of wearing, cut out from any kind of paper we could lay our hands on. I was often told off for that as the resourceful cookie that I was, I'd use anything I could get my hands on, from lining paper for the walls, which we used to soak up as much damp as possible to cardboard – every material was precious in our household. I'd cut up colours until it got so dark that I couldn't see any more because I was completely absorbed in the task. I was always told off for leaving it on the floor.

I didn't have many hobbies, mainly because they were an extra expense, but I was in the Brownies. I made my vow to 'do my best, to do my duty to God and the Queen and to help other people especially those at home'. This was another reason why my conscience was pricked even further whenever I lied on Mom's behalf or bunked school, though at least when I skipped school, I was helping people at home – oh, the moral quandaries for a young kid to get their head around!

Sometimes, we would march up and down the streets with the Scouts, behind the big band. On those days I felt a great sense of pride. Any dead-end kid labels dissolved – no one could differentiate between us in our uniforms. Everyone's parents, including my mom, would come out to watch us. We were all instructed to stand tall, march on and not get distracted by anyone waving and calling to us. I couldn't help but look out for Mom, though. There she was, dressed no differently from all the other housewives, with her hair wrapped in a turban, wearing a pristinely clean pinafore to make sure she didn't show us up. She was beaming away and looked so proud as we came marching by. I couldn't help but instinctively throw my hand up to wave back at her. Brown Owl shot me a stern look, but thankfully I wasn't the only one.

When I was about eight, Auntie Phoebe kindly asked if she could pay for me to have tap dancing lessons. She had a soft spot for me, which Dad didn't take too kindly to. He told her she couldn't show me preferential treatment and would have to pay for Barbara too. So off we went together – as well as being dressed the same, we had to have the same hobbies too! However, we both really enjoyed it. We had red T-bar shoes with silver coloured tap metal plates on the bottom – I loved to hear the sound on the floor following the steps we'd learnt. I was nervous the first lesson as we all stood in a line – I'd never done anything like this before. Of course PE at school was the closest but we were always just in our vest and pants, rather than this fancy footwear. Here, I felt the extra pressure of standing in a line and concentrating, trying my hardest to follow all the steps as the teacher sang, 'Shuffle one, shuffle two, stamp, stamp, shuffle one, shuffle two, stamp, stamp' – it's funny that I can still remember this today. At first I felt silly, but I soon got into it. Barbara and I really looked forward to our one-hour lesson each week and enjoyed seeing our progression as we got better. We used to drive our parents mad, practising the steps at home. Any dreams of taking the world by storm were cut short though when Auntie Phoebe said she could no longer afford the lessons.

But there was still roller-skating at the Embassy on Walford Road as a treat, which all of my siblings loved to do together. We'd go when we could on a Saturday afternoon. The boys used to whizz us around the rink incredibly fast. Barbara and I held onto them and tried to join in. If we fell, we always got up and tried again – my brothers hardwired that mentality into me in many ways. It was so freeing and fun, the closest feeling to flying and a change from the streets at home. As ever, the lads were told to look after me and Barbara. However, they did their best to avoid us if they had their eyes on any girls and didn't want us getting in the way, spoiling their chat-up lines. If there were any boys that we liked, we'd follow them around and try our best to keep up with them. More often than not we'd end up falling over, which was quite a good ploy really because they'd have to help us up and we'd have a little chat in the cafe with them. It's a hobby I used to enjoy with my own kids and grandchildren, up until at least the age of sixty – I'm not quite so nimble anymore! But as was the way, we created a lot of our own entertainment, inspired by our musical idols. The fifties are often celebrated as a time of innocence before the Swinging Sixties kicked into gear and this is reflected in the majority of the music.

I was barely ten when Tommy Steele hit the top spot in the British charts with 'Singin' the Blues'. A wonderful song, it's one that still stands up for me because you can hear all the words – my grandchildren laugh at me when I get so many of the words wrong in today's pop songs. Tommy really did have a lovely clear, rich voice that still resonates years later in my opinion. With lyrics like: 'Well, I never felt more like cryin' all night, 'cause everything's wrong, and nothin' ain't right, without you, you got me singin' the blues' – they ushered in a time when song lyrics were slowly beginning to become more self-reflective and questioning, rather than merely enquiring on the price of a doggy in the window or singing about the sun with his hat on.

Tommy's songs hinted at the dawning of an era when songs would explore darker themes or the pain of unrequited love. None of this really mattered much at the time, of course – Ann, Valerie and I just adored Tommy Steele and his music. And as with everything else, we didn't let a lack of resources thwart our ambitions to form our own rock'n'roll band! We banged on an old saucepan lid or the bottom of saucepans for the drums and we used a comb with paper on it that we blew into to make tunes and made our own fun 'singin' the blues'. We also borrowed Mickey's trumpet when he wasn't around – he would have gone mad if he'd found out.

When we heard that our hero was coming to the Hippodrome we were so excited. Valerie wanted us to embroider 'Tommy Steele' in pink onto purple tops and seeing as sewing wasn't my strong point, Ann helped me out with chain stitch. The Birmingham Hippodrome has gone through many different facelifts but first opened as the tower of varieties and circus at the turn of the last century. I'd never been before but knew it was unlikely to happen and that this would be a rare treat indeed. But I spoke to Mom, who was pregnant at the time (with Philip, I think), and she said if I could run some errands, do some extra chores and help mind the baby she was about to give birth to, I could go. Over the moon with joy, I ran down the entry to the Nees' house to tell Ann and Valerie to book a ticket for me.

When the night finally arrived we were so excited. We walked into town to save money for the bus home – it was about two miles away from Arthur Street. It was incredible to see Tommy Steele in the flesh; I'd only ever heard that beautiful voice before on the wireless or records that Ann and Valerie owned, so to see him up close was spectacular. Along with the other girls we sang our hearts out, and our throats were sore from shouting 'I never felt more like singin' the Blues' and screaming at the tops of our lungs – 'Tommy, we love you – you're the best!' We had to go to the toilet to get a drink of water – our mouths were so dry and we hadn't got the money for a drink. After that, whenever we heard Tommy on the wireless we'd turn the sound up to full blast – it would make a scratchy noise but we never minded.

20

Leaving Childhood Behind and Moving to Sheldon

In a family as big as mine it wasn't always easy to assert your own identity. But my love for Tommy Steele, tap dancing, creating my own dolls and finally getting my own coat (that was completely different from Barbara's!), these were all steps towards me figuring out my own preferences and tastes in life. I was in the process of taking my first few steps into adulthood. It's hard to define when this transition is made – it's gradual, it's subtle, and you don't really notice it until you look back.

Most of the time people tend to romanticise the typical fifties childhood with good reason. We used our imaginations with a freedom I don't think children enjoy today, climbed trees, ripped our clothes, never locked our doors and played out on the streets. And while yes, I cherish those memories, it's rare any childhood passes without an event that adults can't explain or protect them from. The strange, the bizarre, the inexplicable that often comes out of nowhere, yet leaves an indelible mark – a blemish on your childhood that never quite fades and catapults you without warning into unrecognisable territory you were completely unprepared for.

I found this out one evening playing Hide and Seek with my brothers down Arthur Street. In the summer we would often play out till ten at night and it was still quite light too. It was the summer holidays and about eight in the evening. Mom, Dad and our teachers had always warned us 'not to go off with strangers' but even then, we imagined a stranger as a witch, a warlock, an obvious villain that's skulked out of a fairytale. The man who asked Carol and me for directions to Jenkins Street looked nice, pleasant and ordinary enough. It was barely a five-minute walk away – we knew where it was because my brother David went to school there. Besides, he said he was new to the area and would we be so kind as to show him the way since he was lost? We nodded blithely, not thinking much of it all as we set off with him – as far as we were concerned, we were doing a good turn like any decent Brownie would. It'd confuse the lads too, they'd think we'd found a particularly good hiding place.

We walked along beside him towards the top of our road. Alarm bells only started ringing when he mentioned a shortcut he knew – a gully down the side of the road that we knew would be muddy because it had rained in the past few days. We had barely a chance to glance at each other when he grabbed us both and suddenly dragged us into the gully. Of course, it all happened so quickly but it's extraordinary really: the main thing that kept running through my head at the time was, 'Mom will go mad if he breaks the elastic on my knickers, please don't break them'. That was my main concern as we both screamed and yelled at him to stop – even then I had no real comprehension of what he was trying to do. We were both so innocent and it just wouldn't have occurred to us at the age of nine what his intentions were. Yes, we played on the streets, but we weren't streetwise in that sense.

Besides, events like this could never be discussed. They were pushed under the carpet, woven into the 'hush, hush' culture that adults created in their complicit silence, ensuring victims stayed silent too. Not that I could ever have even attempted to put the incident into words. People often ask 'Why did the child not tell?' but I know that I certainly didn't have the words to explain what had happened, let alone how it left me feeling.

I remember he was strong but somehow I got away after I kicked him hard. He was still holding onto Carol while she cried and shouted 'Stop!' but he had a strong grip on her. It sounds clichéd to say, but I ran in a blind panic back down the alley as my flight impulses to survive kicked in – I couldn't bear to contemplate what was happening to my friend as I banged and banged on the door at the bottom of the gulley. An old lady appeared, looking angry and bewildered as she shouted and waved her stick around, yelling, 'What are you up to?' No doubt she'd endured enough nonsense over the years from 'Knock, Knock, Run' games. Her expression changed quite quickly though as she saw I was in an obvious state of distress. I think words such as 'the man tricked us' tumbled from my mouth as I pointed my arm down in the direction of the alley towards the sounds of Carol crying. The lady, God bless her, didn't hesitate in lunging forward fast, as fast as a lady with a walking stick could, hitting the man several times on the back with her stick, all the while shouting: 'Bugger off or I'll fetch the police on you!' He was so distracted that Carol managed to wrestle free and off he ran.

The lady told us to tell our moms but we were so shaken and scared and thought we'd never be allowed out again. Instead we looked at each other and vowed that we would never tell another soul the true facts of what had happened that night. We cut our fingers and became blood sisters to seal the promise, mopping the blood up as we dried our eyes and set off back down the street. But my brothers knew something was up the minute they saw us, shuffling back silently towards them. 'Where were you hiding, where were you hiding?' they pestered us. 'That's for us to know and you to find out,' we replied.

But that was not to be the end of it. Weeks later, I heard a bang on the door and raised voices while I was in bed, drifting off to sleep. Then came the sound of Dad charging up the stairs, shouting: 'I want a word with you, my lady! What have you been up to?' Shaking, I went downstairs, half-knowing what it was about – the memories were still so fresh to me that I was starting to feel all the same emotions.

I saw two policemen standing in our sitting room. Dad looked furiously at me, compounding all my secret fears it had been our fault, that we'd done something to deserve it. Mom looked confused.

I remember that one of the policemen was kind as soon as Dad started to interrogate me about what I'd been up to. He stepped in and said: 'Please, let us deal with this.' They asked Mom to make me a cup of tea and sit me down as they could see I was shaking a lot. I think one of them said: 'She's in shock, fetch a blanket.'

All I could think was that Carol had broken our promise and I was going to be really angry with her when I saw her again. It was all a bit of a blur as they went on to tell me that Carol had been attacked on her way to the chip shop and had told the police it had happened once before and she thought it was the same man. I couldn't believe it, the same man, doing it again? Poor Carol. I was relieved they were being so nice to me but I was still very confused by all the questions. They asked if I could come to the station, do a statement and look at some photos to see if I could identify the attacker. In some ways I was also relieved they said 'attacker' – it helped me feel as though it was less my fault.

So I went to the police station with Mom and Dad. We were there for ages while I did my best to cobble together a description – 'About forty, tall, maybe five feet ten, thin with dark hair and wearing a gabardine raincoat'. I did my best to remember without scaring myself too much, it was hard to revisit all the details. Mom asked if they thought they'd catch him and they said they would 'give it a good try'. Then we were allowed to go home. Dad never made it to the pub that night. We got home late and the lads were full of questions. I really didn't want to talk about it, though.

That night I lay in my bed, unable to sleep, thinking and wondering about the awful details of what could have happened to Carol. I tried everything I could to get it out of my mind and eventually managed to fall asleep, replacing the nasty thoughts with lovely memories of the farm in Devon – the bed all to myself, the food, the fun times with Eileen, all the space we had to run around in outside in the fresh air. Somehow, the cold seemed even worse that night as I covered myself with a coat.

After that I never saw Carol again. I went to call for her but the neighbours said they'd 'done a moonlit flit, shouldn't wonder'. I knew it must have been linked to the man and the attack. Weeks later, I heard my parents talking about that night but they always changed the subject when I came in and never spoke to me directly about it.

That event felt like a turning point to me. Something had changed inside of me: some door had been opened I couldn't bang shut again. Not even making dolls out of cardboard and dressing them with wallpaper could quite shake it for me. I was always in trouble for cutting paper up in the attic and making a mess up there but Mom didn't get cross with me for doing it anymore. I wanted her to be cross with me again, for things to go back to normal somehow. I hoped that when I next played out in the street it would return, that the very action of playing Tig and all those childhood games would shake the thoughts from my head, restoring balance, order and normality. But there were yet more inevitable changes outside of my control, which were to alter our lives more dramatically than I could ever have realised. At the age of eleven, I started my periods. For any young woman it's an important milestone, as well as an ordinary and everyday part of nature and growing up. But it signalled the end of an era, not just for me but for all of us. I'd long outgrown sharing a bed with my brothers but this became ever more apparent by the time I started secondary school and my body was developing.

If you had a girl of eleven sharing a room with older boys, you automatically gained extra points, enough to apply for a bigger house. For nearly a year I'd been sleeping in the single bed downstairs with my parents. This was all taken into consideration at the housing department at Bush House, based on Broad Street in the city centre. Mom was also expecting our little sister Josephine and the house was clearly overcrowded.

It all happened so quickly and I felt very upset by the upheaval at what was already a delicate time. I'd already been at my new senior school at Tilton Road for six months and had settled in and made new friends. But we were moving to a new home in Sheldon, a proper semi-detached house. It was part of a council estate built back in the thirties, one of five large outer-city estates at Quinton, Harborne and Washwood Heath – these neighbourhoods were provided with their own shops, schools and libraries and had a strong community feel. Technically, they were in the suburbs, right at the end of the Coventry Road, about five miles away from Arthur Street, and all but half an hour in the bus. But it might as well have been another world to us. It seemed as though we were out in the country in comparison and it may as well have been, with its landscaped green spaces we had to play in.

The hardest part was saying goodbye to everyone. They all congregated in our courtyard on the day we left – Nancy Nee, Ann, Valerie, the Bottrells, the Ellises and the Griffins. It was a completely fresh start. Mom didn't even want to take anything with her to remind her of the past, so she left the beds and gave away a lot to our neighbours and friends who had been so kind to us. She then washed and scrubbed the front step with carbolic soap within an inch of its life for the very last time – I felt sorry for the poor new buggers who'd be slipping on it as they made their way in!

It was a lot to process – I was leaving, not only my new school but the back-to-back streets which, despite all their poverty and problems, had been the only home I'd ever known. Mom couldn't contain her delight, though: she looked at my teary face and just smiled. She said: 'We will make new friends and our old ones can visit.' But somehow I knew I never would see them again. Even though they were only half an hour away in a car, they seemed to belong to another world now, one that may almost never have existed in some ways. Even the cat we took with us knew it – when we got out of the removal van he scarpered back home, never to be seen again. He was happier chasing rats, mice and spiders, said Mom. We'd had enough of that, though.

Within another ten years Manzoni's full vision would be realised and whole communities would be decimated, along with the houses. Some of them would be packed off into high rises to build new dreams in the sky, often with devastating consequences. This was laid out no more starkly than the mothers who, in a number of incidents in the 1970s, jumped from their windows, sometime with their babies or toddlers, once they'd finally given up on the dreams they'd been told they'd fulfil, up on the 18th floor.

We were very lucky, though. And I realise that even more, looking back. We had everything we'd ever dreamed of in our new home in Sheldon. It was as though Dennis's made-up stories had finally come true – Joey Ellis really had heard us this time, waved his wand and granted all our wishes. There was the sheer size of the place for a start – four bedrooms, unthinkable to us before, with their own walk-in wardrobes. Imagine somewhere proper to keep Dad's silk pyjamas!

Downstairs there was a large sitting room and a smaller one leading off it. We now had that trademark symbol of middle-class respectability – the parlour room to 'receive' guests. And our own front door! No more sharing of walls so thin you could hear the neighbours taking a wee each night. The kitchen was kitted out with a new modern gas cooker, built-in cupboards, draining boards, a fitted table and large cupboard for utensils – everything a family needed to live comfortably. And no more copper brick in the brewus. Now we had something called a utility room, with a new twin tub, another sink and more cupboards. My God, could this mean we were posh now?

There was no central heating but the larger living room had a modern gas fire – a dream come true. In the smaller room was a fireplace where we could have a coal fire too – old habits die hard and all. Mom's days of getting the ashes up in the cold mornings were definitely numbered, though. There was a long hallway leading to the front door and everywhere smelt clean and new. We had our own back door that led out to a big garden, where Mom could finally grow her own flowers and vegetables. Perhaps we could even camp out there in the summer too. There was a veranda with a glass roof, south-west facing, where the sun streamed in. It was as though someone was playing a joke on us.

And our very own outdoor toilet! No more crossing our legs and waiting in a queue for the lav to be free. Not that we would ever use it – to our absolute delight we had our own bathroom upstairs. Finally, our own hot running water and a second toilet – what utter luxury, none of it seemed real! We had to touch the porcelain lid and shiny hanging chain to believe it. We were all completely overcome, no more than Mom though, who gave birth to Josephine a few weeks before her due date.

Yes, the mod cons, the size, the light, the warmth and ease of it all were fantastic. But for me it represented the beginning of a new sense of freedom where we could be ourselves – from the shed in the garden, where Dad could concentrate on his woodwork to Mom marking out her own territory in the garden. And for all of us kids, we now lived in a house that was built with firm foundations, one that was built to last, but ultimately a house that was built to be a home for a family. It was here that we could build upon and work towards fulfilling our dreams.

As the last generation of kids to come out of the back-to-backs we have made history and defied the grim predictions of the naysayers who said we'd amount to little. When you meet all nine of us you wouldn't think we'd been brought up in the tough conditions that we were. Throughout our careers we've always valued and appreciated what we've worked hard for and this has instilled an unwavering sense of inner strength and self-belief within us, a knowledge there's little we can't face or overcome and wherever we are, we can improvise with the resources we have to hand. We can stand proud and say this made us who we are today.

21

Earning My Own Wage as a Hairdresser and Meeting My Husband Ray

I didn't exactly set out to be a hairdresser but looking back, some of the hair disasters we experienced in the back-to-backs may have had something to do with it, not least for poor Mom. As we couldn't afford to get our hair done we used what resources we could to create the most glamorous hairstyles possible – from a hot poker warmed on the fireplace to pipe cleaners. It's a wonder Mom had any hair left after the back-to-backs, not least when one of the neighbours came round to offer a home perm or a 'twink', a popular brand of home perm kit.

She wrapped Mom's lovely, dark hair in pipe cleaners, then twisted it into these awful contraptions to wear all night – Dad hated the smell and was immediately suspicious. When her friend took them out the next day,

Mom screamed in fright to see she'd inadvertently created her very own Afro hairstyle several decades before they properly came into fashion. Dad went mad when he saw it – she was barely recognisable and didn't look like our mom at all! In hindsight, it was definitely a mistake to leave it in overnight.

It lasted ages before it started to grow out – she had to keep cutting it, but it seemed to get even curlier than before. It was a long time before Mom let anyone near her hair again. She didn't really quite trust me enough until I could prove my credentials with a hair salon of my own!

From the age of about thirteen I was determined to start earning my own wage to help out Mom but also to give me more individual freedom of choice – in my own clothes and hairstyles. Perhaps I'd even buy some clothes from an actual shop for a change. One Saturday, I trawled down the Coventry Road and Hay Mills, looking for work, asking in all the salons until I came to one called May Install, named after the woman who owned and ran the business. In her fifties, she was a good-looking woman with dark wavy hair. Though kind, she could be quite strict and formal and wasn't quick to show her warmer side. She was what Mom would call a 'proper lady' – she'd also never married so was labelled with the lovely term 'spinster' too.

She took a shine to me and gave me a Saturday job. It didn't take her long to see I had a strong work ethic and soon she had me doing all sorts – mopping the floors and cleaning the salon from top to bottom, washing towels in her twin tub in the outside shed and hanging out washing on the line. She lived in the flat above the salon and I cleaned that out for her during the holidays, stripped the wallpaper in her rooms and helped her to paint and decorate too. In return, she taught me how to juggle the really important tasks – namely shampooing hair and making a cup of tea.

When I was fifteen and about to leave school (until 1972, fifteen was the age at which you could legally leave school), she called me in to her private office to say she wanted to speak to my dad about an apprenticeship. As she explained, girls normally had to pay for this honour but she knew my parents were too poor to pay. She suggested taking me on for a three-year contract with the possibility of extending it another two years. I was so happy that she had faith in me and wanted to give me a chance, it meant a lot to me. She taught me everything – from cutting to perming, colouring and waving. I worked every day, from 8.30 till 6pm, with Sundays and half a day on Tuesday off, and earned seven shillings and sixpence (37.5p; about £6 today) a week, plus tips.My parents were very pleased and proud of me, and another bonus was that they didn't have to pay for the apprenticeship.

It was extremely hard work standing on my feet all day but I loved it, especially to have my first taste of independence and earn my own wage. My new boss had a nephew called John, who was about thirty when I started working there. He was a lot more laid-back than May and when she was out on a Thursday the atmosphere was a lot more relaxed – he also taught me how to do pin curls, waves, barrel curls, rollers and perming. He loved to do the modern backcombing, which I soon adopted for myself – long gone were the curls! There was another stylist of about twenty-one, second to John, and a girl one year older than me called Sheila. There was also a girl called Anita, who was also doing an apprenticeship – she lived in a big house on the Coventry Road and her dad had paid for her to do it. But although she was posh, it really didn't matter in this brave new world where class structures were slowly dissolving. I was branching out into the world of work, where these differences mattered less – we were judged on our ability to do the job, not the size of our parents' house or whether they kept their own livestock.

Soon I became more confident in experimenting with my own hairstyles – I replaced the unruly curls of my childhood with a sleeker, more sophisticated and stylish backcomb, lacquered and flicked up at the bottom. I experimented with make-up too and learnt how to apply black eyeliner properly, flicking up at the ends.

Next door to the hairdresser's was a butcher's store. When I was about fifteen I used to go in there for May's food shopping. There was a shy, nice-looking lad in there who used to sing along to the tunes on the radio. He could never quite look me in the eye when I asked him for a couple of meat chops and would get quite red and flustered, as did

I. The other butchers would nudge each other whenever I came in and tease him mercilessly. As time went on, he got a little bit more confident and I think he was warming up to asking me out properly. However, the lad's burgeoning career as a butcher as well as his brief flirtations with me were cut short when the business closed down and was transformed into a men's tailor's. Who knows, it may well have been this enforced change in career direction that led to this promising young butcher pursuing another career path for he was none other than Gerry Marsden from Gerry and the Pacemakers.

This twist of fate also led to the most important encounter of my life. It just so happened that one of the men working on the building site next door was my future husband Ray. He'd recently finished a six-month season at Butlins working as a general labourer, turning over the chalets. He was worn out – not so much from the work as it turns out but the endless boozing, drinking and dancing into the late hours. During this stint he got to know one particular drummer who was playing for the holiday camp's resident band. It was none other than Ringo Starr, with whom he used to shoot pool into the early hours. Of course Ray had no idea then of the hugely important role his friend would go on to play in the history of British rock'n'roll. But that was not to be their last meeting – less than a year later, The Beatles were headlining a club called The Ritz Ballroom in King's Heath, a suburb of South Birmingham. In its glory days throughout the sixties bands as big as The Rolling Stones, The Kinks and Pink Floyd also played there.

It was 1962 and The Beatles had just released 'Love Me Do'. Everyone was dancing away to the resident house band Second City Sound, followed by Joe Brown & The Bruvvers. But Ray never forgets that when The Beatles came on and opened with 'Love Me Do', the crowd instantly stopped moving and stood listening, so mesmerised were they by the quality of the music. They were on the cusp of international fame but weren't as yet so far removed from their fans, to the extent that Ray ended up next to Ringo in one of the urinals. He looked over at him and said: 'Oh alright, what you doing 'ere?'

'I've come to see you, mate,' replied Ray. He ended up meeting the rest of the band and buying them all a round of 'mild' in the bar upstairs – a decision he finds hilarious, seeing as they went on to become millionaires.

So, after a brief stint mixing with mega stars, Ray came back down to earth, working on the construction site for the new tailor's shop. It was here that he caught the eye of nearly all the girls that I worked with – from me, the apprentice, to all the senior girls. Whenever we went outside to dry off the towels used for women's perms we'd hang them on the line and all sneak a look at him as we pretended to be busy pegging them up. In fact, towel hanging suddenly became one of our most favourite tasks, especially when Ray was burning rubbish out the back – anything to catch a glimpse of him as our faces peeped out between the towels. With his dark wavy hair and Teddy Boy quiff, we all thought he was absolutely gorgeous! I'm sure he knew our game as we trotted out endlessly with yet more towels and definitely caught my eye a few times as he stood stripping all the shelves out of the shop, covered in smoke. At the time I'd had very little experience of boys other than a brief flirtation with a lad called George and that was only because I was impressed by his motorbike – once I realised what sitting on the back of one did to my hair, I went right off the idea!

One day, Annette, who was far more brazen than me, strode out into the courtyard and asked him straight out which one of us he liked best. We'd all become a bit bored with the towel-twitching carry-on and wanted a straight answer. Ray looked at the four of us, thought for a minute and then said 'The little dark one' while pointing furtively at me. I was absolutely gobsmacked – this gorgeous lad liked me!

Eventually he asked me out and we arranged to meet outside The Locarno in Hurst Street, which was opened by the Mecca Leisure Group in 1960. Despite its rather typical concrete sixties exterior, it had a glitzy and glamorous interior – plush red velvet seating and gold-edged mirrors. Ray kept me waiting at least half an hour, though. I was just preparing to leave in a huff when I saw him striding down the streets towards me. His cheeky smile stopped me right in my tracks. 'Ooh, he's gorgeous!' I thought. I could barely stop staring at him as he wandered up to me. All was forgiven when I saw those twinkling eyes and his lovely thick hair – the two most important assets to me! I didn't realise it at the time but his hair was actually coated in lard – a substitute for Brylcreem and what all the Teddy Boys used. Fortunately though, this was not to be the night I ran my hands through it. Our date was not to be at The Locarno, though – a disappointment, to say the least. Instead, we got on the less-than-glamorous number 48 bus through the rundown area (at the time) of Balsall Heath through to Ray's favourite pub, the Horseshoe in Warstock.

I never once thought that I'd end up marrying him, I just felt pleased as punch he'd turned up and couldn't wait to tell the girls on Monday that I'd bagged a date. I wore a little red skirt, a blue and white shirt with a red pinafore and matching red tie – later on, Ray said he wasn't too sure about the outfit because he thought I looked a bit like a schoolgirl! We had some communication problems in the early days too, of course. One night, sitting in the back row at the cinema, Ray turned to look at me romantically as though about to kiss me. He then burst out laughing. I was really upset for the rest of the film and on the way home. Turns out, he'd just been laughing at the film we were watching – it was a Charlie Drake comedy after all. Thankfully, none of these incidences dampened the romance between us, not even Ray's lard-coated hair.

By the time we were eighteen we were engaged. Ray bought me a solitaire diamond on a twisted gold band for £48, a king's ransom at the time. To celebrate our engagement, Mom and Dad booked their favourite pub in Sheldon – St Bernard's Grange or simply 'The Grange'. Dad couldn't resist the urge to get up on the mic and sing 'True Love' to Mom. It was another three years until we were married – the day after my twenty-first birthday on 25 March 1967.

Life didn't suddenly become a bed of roses when I left the back-to-backs and believe me, there have been many times when I've desperately wished Dennis could conjure up Joey Ellis again with his magic wand, just to make it all alright. It's been a rollercoaster to say the least and as many other married couples will testify, Ray and I have experienced our ups and downs, but we have survived. Earlier this year (2017), we celebrated our golden wedding anniversary, happy to be surrounded by our beautiful children, grandchildren and great-grandchildren.

As Harry Lauder sings in 'Keep Right On to the End of the Road' – Birmingham City Football Club's well-loved anthem – the road through life can be a long one, full of both joys and sorrows. But it's courage that keeps you walking on, until you reach the end. There was a time when, as a child, I thought Arthur Street was one of the only roads I was ever destined to walk down. Its terraced uniformity of crumbling houses seemed to shrug under the weight of the smog some days, as if to say to us 'Don't bother aiming higher.' But we did all choose to find different roads, and we did dare to aim higher. Some of these roads weren't so far away – I loved the Coventry Road as a kid and still do, not least because it's where I met my beloved Ray. But I've been fortunate enough to venture further, too, to places where I never dreamt my feet would tread – as well as raise two children, own six salons and a property in Spain along the way.

The Arthur Street of the 1950s is long gone. Pleasant, inoffensive looking cul-de-sacs (the term also means dead-end, of course) and bungalows have replaced the back-to-backs. History may have been too embarrassed to leave them standing, but the street I grew up in will forever have a special place in my heart, along with the memories of the people that made it home – Mr Bottrell's welcoming, calm face as we went begging for a tanner, Nancy Nee's turban barely askew as she delivered yet another baby, or Mrs Beighton beaming at Dennis as she slipped another few penny sweets into our tuck boxes. They all stay with me, as I continue on down this road, looking to the future but always with a thankful and grateful nod back to the past.